WHEN GOD SEEMS FAR AWAY

When God Seems Far Away

Biblical insight
for common
depression

Mark R. Littleton

Harold Shaw Publishers
Wheaton, Illinois

Cover Photo: Edward Kumler

ISBN 0-87788-938-4

Library of Congress Cataloging-in-Publication Data

Littleton, Mark R., 1950–
    When God seems far away.

    1. Consolation.   I. Title.
BV4905.2.L52   1987   231.7   87–4701
ISBN 0-87788-938-4

---

96   95   94   93   92   91   90   89   88   87
10   9   8   7   6   5   4   3   2   1

Contents

JOB

Job, how did you do it?
You've put quite a crink
in the established repertoire.
I'd have hauled off and socked someone
about the time the camels were stolen.
But you?

Job, I'm curious.
Why didn't you curse God?
You could have repented afterwards.
I've done that.
I've even given up the faith,
threatened God,
told him to get out of my life.
But you?
You just sat there,
scraping the boils and talking theology.

Job, I'd like to meet you.
Ask a few pointed questions.
See your face.
Find out
if there's even the least
little bitterness lurking
deep down there
somewhere.
Come on.
Tell the truth.

Job, I can't get around it.
You made it.
You set the world on end,
proved your faith like no one since.
Please tell me how.
I need to know.

Not that I'm into it as deep as you.
If all those things had happened to me,
I'd have checked out long ago.
No, it's just that
it's so easy to give up.
Daily. Minute by minute.

And you didn't.
What can I say, Job?
Thanks.
Only thanks.

Mark R. Littleton

Introduction

*T*here comes a time for every Christian when God seems far away. It's not the usual kind of test we often experience—everyday problems or difficulties. For during such times, God often seems especially near, real, and sympathetic.

Nor is it an emotional tailspin. You've been depressed before. You know what it's like to feel "down" and alone. But in the past, it always passed—quickly and forgettably.

No, during this period it's like God Himself has deserted you. He's vanished. Poof! A week ago, He was so real. Peace like a river. Joy like a fountain. But now it's all gone. He's gone. You've never felt this alone in your life.

Has it happened to you? Is it happening now?

Let me describe such a period.

You were wondrously converted only a short time ago. Maybe

six months. Maybe a year. Maybe two or three. Or maybe you were converted long ago, as a child, but only recently has God become the passion of your life. Whatever your case, Jesus has seemed so near. Often you wonder how you missed it for so many years. Sometimes you even ask yourself, "How did I make it without Him for all that time?"

Your prayer is like drinking eggnog—smooth, refreshing, revitalizing. Sometimes an inner jolt of joy resounds in your heart.

When you read His word, the verses bound off the page. You claim them like a child gripping a homerun ball at Little League.

In church, the choir thrills you, the pastor's words ignite you, the fellowship is sweet. You love everyone. Everything is new, beautiful, resplendent.

You walk barefoot on grass and it's as though you've discovered the new joy therapy. You walk into the local market and the colors leap out at you. Momentarily, you stand in awe and wonder and quietly thank the Lord for the gift of sight. Jesus is so great, true, alive, and present, you sometimes break into song or a shout of triumph: "I'm so glad You came into my life!" You want to tell everyone about Him. It's so natural, you don't even feel afraid.

Even temptation is no problem. You feel protected, enwrapped in a holy glow of power. You tell yourself, "Nothing will ever make me unhappy again."

Then something happens.

At first, it's difficult to describe. Everything that seemed so new suddenly looks dull again. But you shrug it off. "Just a bad day, I guess." Yet, it goes on. Not just a day. A week. A month.

You feel as though you're stuck in a slump. "I feel dried out," you tell a friend.

Your friend just says, "Pray about it. The Lord'll make it right." But when you pray, the Lord doesn't even seem to hear. Nothing happens.

Then church ceases to excite you. You start to notice the gossip. People bother you. You begin to complain. Church becomes a matter of duty now.

Even listening to the once thrilling messages is difficult. You can't concentrate. You think about everything but the subject at hand. You worry a lot. Sometimes anxiety strikes like a branding iron. You flinch and pretend everything's okay, but inside you're deeply disappointed. "Something's wrong," you tell yourself. But everyone else seems so "with it." You're afraid to let your real feelings show.

It becomes harder and harder to read the Bible. You try. "Why aren't I interested any more?" you ask yourself. You feel guilty.

Old habits and sins you'd conquered in the first few months of your walk are popping up everywhere. The old pattern of anger emerges. You're irritable. You mouth off to your husband, wife, teacher, or your parents. You tend to be touchy.

Then something more sinister happens: you begin having doubts. "Am I really a Christian?"

Something deep down inside responds, "It was all just a phase. You'll get over it." You reel in horror at the thought. But it bugs you.

Soon a creeping, gripping discouragement begins to enfold you. "Other Christians seem to have it so together," you tell yourself. "But I'm such a hypocrite. God can't love me very much, the way I act."

Still you put on a smile and tack on your testimony. Inside, though, you scream at God. "What have I done? Have I sinned against You, Lord? Please forgive me. Show me what I'm doing wrong. Please get me out of this."

Then other trials start. Things go wrong. You can't pay important bills. Maybe you even lose your job and can't find one, even though you pray daily.

Sometimes there are physical problems. An illness. A weakening. Mental confusion. Neuroses. But your doctors can't find anything wrong. They run all sorts of tests. One doctor suggests counseling.

You start to pray for a physical healing. Though you consider yourself rather conservative theologically, you begin reading books by faith healers. You even attend a few services. One time you go forward to be anointed and prayed over. But nothing changes.

The darkness within you fumes into stagnant clouds of confusion.

Then a new notion strikes. "Does God really exist? Is this all just a fantasy? Am I deluded?"

You shudder and force it out of your mind. But it hammers away, like the tick of a clock. Yet you know you can't give up. "I've got to find out," you say. "I'll study. I'll pray. O God, please open my eyes."

But even the verses you used to claim no longer work. God is silent. Prayers are left unanswered. You plead for a sign, for peace, a way out. But it feels as though God has deserted you.

You run from friend to friend, church to church, book to book looking for an answer—the secret that will jar you out of this nightmare. But it goes on and on. A year. Two years.

At times you think about suicide. But you're afraid. You're convinced if you did that, you'd be sentencing yourself to eternal hell. It's the only thing that keeps you from leaping over that brink.

At other times, you plead with God to kill you. "What use am I like this, Lord?"

You begin to feel God has rejected you and that you've committed the unpardonable sin. So you search your heart and life. But you can't find anything. You scour away at your soul, searching for that one sliver of sin you committed somewhere that brought on all this. You confess everything, even things you don't think were wrong. You go to others and confess trivial things. "I'm sorry I forgot to say thank you. Will you forgive me?" But even that doesn't change your situation. The suffering goes on.

Sometimes you take long walks in the park and weep. "Why can't I get out of this, God? What's wrong with me?"

You wonder if you've lost your mind, become a schizophrenic. "Why won't You heal me, Lord?" You go to church hoping that the pastor will say some magic word that will change everything. But after each service you're even more hopeless than before.

You even try to pretend. "I'll think positively," you tell yourself. That lasts an hour.

"I'll memorize verses till I get out of this," you say. You

memorize hundreds. No change.

"I'll pray it through!" you shout. You get on your knees and pray four hours straight, longer than you ever have before in your life. You only feel worse.

Sometimes you threaten God. "I'll go get drunk," you tell Him. "I'll shoot somebody." But you know it's foolishness.

The pain just goes on and on. "When will this end?" you ask over and over. "What are You trying to teach me, Lord?" But no answers come.

Every day you give up. "I can't take this any longer."

Then every day you resolve, "No, I can't give up. I can't stop being a Christian."

But your heart is screaming. "Help, Lord. What's wrong? Why is this happening?"

Heaven is silent as midnight. The blackness in your heart only widens. Soon you're convinced it will swallow you, and you'll do something drastic.

Have you been there? Are you there? If so, then this book is for you. We're going to look not only at *why* this happens to Christians, but also at *how to cope* in the midst of it.

Be sure about one thing though. If it has not happened to you, if it is not happening now, there is a good chance it *will* happen—if Jesus plans to employ you to do a great work in His name.

You may be on the brink of one of the greatest transforming acts of the Spirit in your life.

1
God's
Vanishing
Act

*F*or me, a period like that described in the introduction came during my third year in seminary. I had returned from the greatest summer of my life as a pastoral intern at a church in Hershey, Pennsylvania. At my departure, there were so many tears, so many heartfelt hugs and bursts of love, so many gifts pressed upon me, into my pockets and through the mail that I rejoiced in the Lord for days afterward.

I arrived at school full of expectation. Two courses I would take were taught by marvelous profs with a gift for keeping you interested. I was excited, motivated, jubilant, ready for the grind and the glory.

But that first week, something strange happened. I was sitting in our dormitory watching a friend as he and his new fiancée perused pictures from the previous summer. They laughed,

talked in furtive whispers, and gazed into one another's eyes—
you know. They were in love. Suddenly, I found myself fighting
a ream of jealous messages as they tangled and twisted inside
my mind. But I shrugged it all off. "God'll bless me with a wife
someday," I told myself.

Yet, somehow from that moment something went awry within
me. A blackness seemed to envelop my heart. At first I thought
it was just a little downer from being single, without immediate
plans for marriage, and no present partner even for a date. But
over the next week, my inner feelings plummeted into a cavern
of anxiety and depression. I knew this was far more than a bit
of jealousy and depression over my loneliness. But I had no
name for it other than "the blues."

In my classes I became preoccupied, unable to shake off a
confusion of thoughts and worries that bubbled into my mind
like poisonous gas. I couldn't understand what was happening.
Ever since I'd become a Christian over three years earlier, joy,
peace, happiness, and unlimited health found its way to my door
and never had to knock twice. I'd always considered myself
specially blessed. While other students pored over the books, I
got A's without burning a drop of midnight oil. While other friends
battled financial blowouts and problems, I simply cruised along.
Many times money arrived anonymously in my seminary mailbox.
Other times friends or my church from back home sent funds.
Or I discovered an occasional odd job that paid well. I always
received the funds I needed without even asking. Worry was
rare. But now I was worrying nonstop.

By the end of that first week, I was frazzled. For the first
time in my life, I seriously wished to die. I even gazed despon-
dently at the gas jets in our suite, thinking that might be the
way out of this. Though I shook such thoughts off, they were
troubling. This wasn't the teenage blues or the college doldrums.
I was consciously plotting my funeral.

Meanwhile, my feelings were trampling me. I went to a church
elder and told him what was happening. He said he'd pray, and
he sent over another elder in our church who was studying
counseling. After talking for several hours with him, he told me

that the problem might be biochemical. He suggested I see one of the professors on our campus who was also a practicing psychiatrist. He assured me, "He can prescribe some medicine that'll shoot you right out of this. You'll be back to yourself in a week."

I made an appointment and showed up the next day. Medicine was prescribed. I took it. And waited.

In the meantime, other disasters crunched into my psyche. The tension in my arms became so taut my handwriting looked scrawly and stiff, the way my grandmother wrote when she was suffering from severe arthritis. Concentration was impossible. Hangups from the years before my conversion assaulted me in armies. Shame that I had seen a psychiatrist clobbered me daily. I resolved that as soon as the medicine got me out of my condition, I'd stop taking it and stop seeing him.

But nothing changed.

I would take long walks pouring out my feelings to the Lord. But there was no release as there had been in earlier days. The Lord seemed to have vanished.

One night—only weeks after the original strike of depression —I tearfully asked my roommate of two years, "Do you really believe there's a God?" Before this, he'd considered my bout with depression a passing feeling. Now he was worried. He got on the phone and called another prof.

I was desperate and spelled out the story to him over the phone. Immediately, he began grilling me about demon-possession. He advised me to confess to the Lord any involvement with so-called supernatural experiences. Here I was, already convinced I was a nut case, and he was suggesting I was demon-oppressed and possibly possessed! Now I was not only depressed, but terrified. One doctor was talking about this lasting as long as six months!

Over the next weeks I dropped one course, plodded to my other classes bored and fearful, slept late repeatedly, and began cutting any class that began before 11 a.m. I wrote in a journal, "I feel as though barbed wire is being jerked through my veins."

Each night I began to suffer from weird dreams and nightmares, awaking in a sweat, unable to return to sleep. Later, when it wasn't nightmares, it would be a sudden jerking and stretching of my limbs. I'd awake with a start five or ten times a night. I remember asking the Lord the first time it happened, "What new plague has come upon me?"

Maybe this sounds a bit melodramatic or at least over-dramatized. But at the time, the psychic pain was so great I thought about little except suicide or healing. In the meantime, I began questioning everything about my faith. Was there a God? How could Jesus be God? Is the Bible really the Word of God? How do we know? Did Jesus really rise from the dead?

These were truths I'd never questioned as a Christian. But suddenly I was plunged into a dramatic search for faith, answers, hope, and life. Nothing seemed to work anymore. Not prayer. Not scripture. Not church. Not friends. I didn't think I could last through each day. But somehow, during that time, I muddled through two and a half years of it, finding only occasional islands of peace in the midst of a raging inner storm.

Another One Who Knew

There are others who seem to know much about this experience of God vanishing. C.S. Lewis spoke of it in his insightful book, *The Screwtape Letters*. Screwtape, an upper echelon demon, tells his, disciple, Wormwood (a mere tempter) that Christians tend to go through "peaks and troughs" spiritually. That is, there are exciting periods when God seems so real and present that joy jets through their hearts like a geyser, especially at the beginning of their walk with Jesus. But then the troughs come. During these periods the Christian becomes numb, dry, often wondering if everything isn't a cosmic mistake. Lewis calls this the "Law of Undulation."

Lewis writes that both God and Satan can use this natural human tendency to their own ends. Screwtape says of God, "It may surprise you to learn that in His efforts to get permanent possession of a soul, He relies on the troughs even more than on the peaks; some of His special favorites have gone through longer and deeper troughs than anyone else" (p. 45).

4

What's it like? Screwtape explains. At the beginning of our Christian walk, "He (God) will set them (us) off with communications of His presence which, though faint, seem great to them, with emotional sweetness, and easy conquest over temptation. But He never allows this state of affairs to last long. Sooner or later He withdraws, if not in fact, at least from their conscious experience, all those supports and incentives. He leaves the creature to stand up on its own legs—to carry out from the will alone duties which have lost all relish. It is during such tough periods, much more than during the peak periods, that it is growing into the sort of creature He wants it to be" (pp. 46-47).

I recall reading that passage early in my battle with depression. Suddenly, the lights snapped on. I knew I was in a trough. But I didn't know when it would end, or whether it would end. It was somewhat comforting to know I wasn't the only one, that I wasn't some unique mental basket case not even God could help. But the pain was excruciating.

That's the frustration of trough periods. You cry, "When is this going to end, Lord? Why are You doing this to me?" And heaven is silent and dank as an April morning.

Is It Scriptural?
But is what I'm going through confirmed in Scripture?

Many of Scripture's writers speak of this sudden disappearance of God—and the sudden appearance of catastrophes, persecutions, illnesses, and crises.

When the angel of God appeared to Gideon, as he beat a sheaf of wheat in a winepress—presumably to save a few kernels from the marauding Midianites—Gideon's first question was, "If the Lord is with us, why then has all this happened to us?" (Judges 6:13). To be sure, Israel had shuffled off into idolatry. But Gideon was a godly man. Why was he going through this agony? God seemed far away to Gideon.

David, while fleeing from Saul, experienced these troughs many times. In Psalm 13:1, he cries, "How long, O Lord? Wilt Thou forget me forever? How long wilt Thou hide Thy face from me?" Once the Lord was near and warm as a blanket. But now

David couldn't find a rag of hope anywhere.

Paul knew this desolation as well. In 2 Corinthians 12, he wrote that God gave him a "thorn in the flesh" (12:7). This was to keep him from becoming proud about certain revelations he'd received. This was so painful that Paul pleaded three times with God to remove it. But God replied, "My grace is sufficient for you, for power is perfected in weakness" (12:9).

Even Jesus experienced that sudden aloneness and separation from God. On the cross, He cried out, "My God, my God, why hast Thou forsaken me?" (Matthew 27:46). The word "forsaken" pictures an utter and complete desolation, a desertion—the same way a child feels when he finds himself lost in the department store and looks up to find only strange faces and uncomprehending eyes.

An Illustration from Nature

One of Scripture's most graphic pictures of this sudden departure from intimacy comes from Deuteronomy 32:11. "Like an eagle that stirs up its nest, that hovers over its young, He spread His wings and caught them, He carried them on His pinions." Moses was speaking about a phenomenon he must have observed in his many years as a shepherd—the way an eagle trains its young to fly. What he was describing are the steps a parent eagle takes to get the eaglet to leap into the air, flap its wings, and fly off to adventure.

Notice that he says the eagle "stirs up its nest." To understand this, we have to see how an eagle prepares its nest before laying its eggs. When it first forms the nest, the eagle places it high in a tree or crag in the mountains. It uses large sticks, leaves, cloth, things it finds on the ground. Yet, as it carefully constructs this home, in the depression of the nest—where the young will first live and grow—it weaves a bed of brambles, sharp sticks, stones, bones, and other strange but sharp objects. Over this prickly bottom it lays a mat of furs, leaves, and even feathers plucked from its own breast. This done, it lays the eggs in the soft, warm bed, sits on them, and waits for them to hatch.

When the eaglet finally cracks its way out of the egg, it finds itself in a cozy bed, without worry or care. There it is fed, till it grows a splendid feathered covering, three to six months later. Now the eaglet is ready for its first big test. Will it fly?

We might think Pa Eagle would just explain to his sons and daughters that they were made for flying and then send them off into the blue yonder. But the little eaglet looks around at its nest and muses, "I'm quite happy here. There's no need for this flying bit."

That's when Ma and Pa go into action. They "stir up the nest," as Moses says. Suddenly, the eaglet's parents go from friendly to fierce. They fly at the nest ripping out the cozy bottom lining. Instantly, all those brambles and stickers are exposed. When the eaglet tries to sit back, a needle punctures his behind. As he dashes around, his legs are scraped, and he falls beak down into a firethorn patch. His face is bleeding now, and he's looking at Ma and Pa, screaming, "What's going on? What did I do wrong? Don't you like me anymore?"

Ma and Pa say nothing. They simply wait, hovering a short distance away.

So the little eaglet finally hops up to the edge of the nest and peers out. 250 feet straight down! Suddenly he's dizzy. "Better get back in the nest." But it's uncomfortable there, too. So he grips the sticks on the edge of the nest and waits. After awhile he says, "This isn't too bad. I'll just stay here."

Then he notices he's hungry. When he looks up, Pa has just torn into a beak-watering trout he's gotten from the local stream. "Can I have a piece?" asks the eaglet.

Pa has suddenly gone deaf.

"Hey! This is your son! Can I have a piece?"

Pa just chomps into the fish flanks and remarks to his wife, "This is the best trout I ever had." After this Pa Eagle's energy returns. He flies at the eaglet, beating him with his wings.

"What are you doing?" shrieks the eaglet. "You're hurting me!"

But Pa just flails away.

As the eaglet huddles and scampers about, trying to avoid

the powerful wing jabs, he careens closer to the edge. Suddenly the eaglet lifts a wing. He tries to deflect the father with his claws. Now he's losing his balance.

Oh no! He's over the edge. He's falling. He flails at the air with his wings. The wind howls through his ears. He's tumbling, rolling, flapping without even knowing why. The ground leaps up to meet him.

But suddenly, Pa goes into action again. With a great whoosh he swoops down and catches the eaglet on his back, "carrying him on his pinions," as Moses says again.

The eaglet's eyes are popping now. When Pa returns him to the nest, he's sure he'll never try that one again. But they go through the same process again and again until that eaglet flies.

We're Like That Eaglet

This period in the eagle's life when Ma and Pa Eagle seem to get mean is similar to a time in the Christian life when God seems to vanish. The parent eagles are doing everything they can to make the eaglet so miserable that ultimately he'll try to fly. That's what we know as the "troughs" in our walk with Jesus. These times are often subtle—with no apparent outer pain. But they are characterized by deep inner turmoil. Or, like Joni Eareckson Tada and others who have suffered physically, emotionally, *and* spiritually, they can be accompanied by excruciating pain.

Christians can experience this strange disappearance of the Lord's presence while going through marital strife, financial blowouts, persecution, loss of a friend or relative, and the loss of a job. Or it might be less concrete experiences such as a period of spiritual dryness, emotional instability, deep doubt about biblical truth or one's salvation, and uncertainty about what to do with your life. Whatever the case, it will be a time when God will seem far away. You can't seem to reach Him. You know He's there for He said, "I will never desert you, nor forsake you." But it feels and looks like He has done just that.

The Ultimate Example

There is one other person in Scripture who endured a time like this with all its stark realism, pain, and glory: Job. His story will provide the truths that help us stand during this darkest of all the trials of our lives. In the chapters ahead, we'll look at his experience as well as my own and others' experiences. From them, I hope to offer you not only great confidence as you plod through your own darkness, but also joy and peace in the midst of it.

Things to Think About or Discuss:

1. Have you ever felt that during a period of your life God had vanished? What was it like? What did you think and feel during that period? Are you going through it now?

2. Consider several people from Scripture—Moses, Abraham, Jonah, Habakkuk, Gideon, Peter, Paul, Jesus. Can you think of instances where God seemed far away to them? In what situations? Do these biblical characters provide any insight through the recorded events or letters?

3. In the passage about the eagle stirring up its nest, do you see this as a valid argument? Are there other examples in nature that you know of where animals or birds use pain to stimulate growth?

4. If someone came to you and spilled out a story of pain and hopelessness, what Scriptures would you turn to for help? What words of assurance might you give?

2
Before the Pain Starts

When a sick man goes to a doctor, any good doctor wants to know what preceded the illness. "What did you eat? Where had you gone? Did anything unusual happen the last few weeks?" He asks some very personal questions so that he can properly diagnose his patient's problem.

The Book of Job is similar. Through understanding what happened before Job's dramatic disasters, we can make the proper application to our own lives. Job's problems didn't arise simply because God or Satan dropped a bomb upon his otherwise tranquil and holy existence. Nor was the carnage only the result of a whimsical contest between God and Satan. There are clues within the book and before the attack of Satan that provide insight into why God allowed it all to happen. Those insights can help us understand our own battles.

Job: The Man Who Plodded Through Darkness

As a book, Job is difficult to understand. I've read it many times over the last twelve years. But only after numerous "dark" experiences have I begun to crack the door on its real depth. The story often fails to excite, move, or instruct us until we've gone through the same valley Job did.

The book begins with the story of Job's initial sufferings (Job 1 and 2). Three friends (Eliphaz, Bildad, and Zophar) hear of Job's calamity and come to comfort him. For the next twenty-nine chapters they talk, argue, accuse, and very nearly curse this pathetic sufferer. Then a second younger man, Elihu, offers his own thoughts on Job's problem from chapters 32–37. And finally in chapters 38–41 God speaks from the whirlwind and answers Job's challenges.

But who was the man, Job? He was a person, someone who felt the dust between his toes, sang songs by the campfire, and wept as he peered into the eyes of his first newborn babe. If we can discover how he was like and unlike us, we can begin to identify with his struggle, his pain, his hope, and his fear.

Though he probably lived before Abraham, perhaps as early as 2500 B.C., he was a man of wide spiritual dimensions.

Blameless and Upright

The text begins by saying Job was "blameless, upright, fearing God and turning away from evil" (1:1). That he was "blameless" means no man found fault with him. Though he may have had enemies, their opposition was unjustified. If he sinned against anyone, he always made it right with an apology or a gift of restitution. Job lists some of his marvelous deeds to his neighbors in chapter 29. He says,

> When I went out to the gate of the city, when I took my seat in the square; the young men saw me and hid themselves, and the old men arose and stood. The princes stopped talking, and put their hands on their mouths; the voice of the nobles was hushed, and their tongue stuck to their palate. For when the ear heard, it called me blessed; and when the eye saw,

it gave witness of me, because I delivered the poor who cried for help, and the orphan who had no helper. The blessing of the one ready to perish came upon me, and I made the widow's heart sing for joy. I put on righteousness, and it clothed me, my justice was like a robe and turban. I was eyes to the blind, and feet to the lame. I was a father to the needy, and I investigated the case which I did not know. And I broke the jaws of the wicked, and snatched the prey from his teeth (7–18).

It may sound a bit arrogant, even haughty, but clearly Job was some fellow. The "Citizen of the Year" award, a few Presidential Medals of Honor, and even a Nobel Peace Prize would have found their way to his mantle. When Job spoke, everyone listened. When he walked into a room, every head turned and gazed in wonder and admiration. They loved him, revered him. He was as good a neighbor as anyone could ask for.

But he was more than merely good in the eyes of men. He was "upright"—God's own assessment of Job was that Job's heart was clean. When God examined him, He found a man who recognized his sinful condition, put his trust in the Lord, and walked before God with integrity and faith. When he stumbled, he took the right steps to be cleansed. When he succeeded, he thanked the Lord on bent knee. When God took his success away, he still bowed before Him and said, "Blessed be the name of the Lord" (1:21). This wasn't merely hype. Job was the real thing. He had the right stuff. Jesus would never have called him a whitewashed tomb. He was a bloodwashed and bloodbought saint who won both man's and even God's admiration.

Wealthy

Job was also wealthy. He had great herds and multitudes of servants. He was "the greatest of all the men of the East" (1:3).

Again, this isn't biblical hyperbole. Job was hard-working, wise, self-controlled, seeking to do his best. While it's true that God blessed him and even placed a "hedge" about him protecting him from every spiritual and physical enemy, no man gains God's blessing on hot air. Job recognized his responsibility and arose at 5:30 a.m. without flinching.

At the same time, he was no lover of money. In chapter thirty-one, he even pronounced a vivid curse upon himself if he ever came to love money more than God (vv. 24–29). Plainly, he had the right attitude toward his wealth.

Heart Faith

More importantly, Job's faith was a "heart faith." In 1:5, the author indicates that Job made sacrifices to God for his sons and daughters. Why? Job said, "Perhaps my sons have sinned and cursed God in their hearts." Notice that he wasn't concerned only with *externals,* but with *internals* as well. He made sure their hearts were covered and sin was atoned for. Clearly, Job understood that mere keeping of rules doesn't impress God. It is the heart that His eyes light upon.

Self-Sacrificing

Job was self-sacrificing, selfless, giving to others. Some might think he was simply out to protect himself, making sure his world remained intact. But in chapters twenty-nine and thirty-one Job indicated that he practiced the truth. He didn't lust after other women (31:1–3). He never lied to others (31:5–8). He didn't commit adultery (31:9–11). He ruled his slaves with kindness and justice (31:13–15). He never oppressed the poor (31:16–30) and even went out of his way to give to orphans and widows (29:12–16). He stood for justice and fought evil everywhere he found it (29:17). He never rejoiced when wrong came upon others (31:29–37)—even his enemies.

Who hasn't struggled with such difficult issues? Who hasn't failed? Yet not even God contradicts Job's statements. Job was a decent, good, kind, loving man.

A Good Relationship with God

Job had a highly developed and mature relationship with God. When the first series of calamities came upon Job from Satan in chapter one, what was his response? Bitterness? Anger?

Complaining? Amazingly not. He said, "Naked came I from my mother's womb, and naked I shall return there. The Lord gave and the Lord has taken away. Blessed be the name of the Lord" (1:21). Wrapped up in such a statement is an incredible understanding of God—His sovereignty, power, wisdom, goodness, and love—as well as an astonishing personal humility, gratitude, and submission.

Ask yourself what your response to calamity is. I've heard myself screech, "Why are You doing this to me, God? What did I do to deserve this?" on many occasions. Yet the author indicates no such words fell from Job's lips. He "did not sin nor did he blame God" after Satan's first onslaught (1:22). And even when Job's body was smitten with sores and boils and he collapsed on an ash heap to scratch himself with a broken piece of pottery, the author says again, "In all this Job did not sin with his lips" (2:10).

Not a curse, not a blasphemy, not even a complaint (initially) do we hear from this godly man. Certainly this was no ordinary saint. Job was the kind of person God Himself would call "worthy," if He ever called any human worthy.

Does It Add Up?

When you look at these qualities, it seems remarkable that calamity could have struck Job's life. "Isn't he a perfect example of the kind of person God blesses?" If anyone was set up for success, Job was. Frankly, it doesn't seem to add up. Job had everything going for him.

But it's often at just such a time that God starts to seem far away and then vanishes. "Everything was going so well," we say. "Now this." We were solving problems. We were growing, changing. We could see the Lord at work in our lives in a multitude of ways. We even began to wonder if it could get any better. Then the bottom cracks open and we plummet into the volcano!

It was exactly like that for me. When my own depression slammed into my life that September at seminary, I had just come off the best summer of my life. For the past three years I'd practiced a rigorous regimen of Bible study and Bible memory, awaking early each morning to spend time in the Word and prayer. It seemed I had not only journeyed from faith to greater faith, but from jubilation to greater jubilation. Often I remarked to others, "Walking with Jesus just gets better and better. Life is an adventure." I was excited, happy, motivated, unswerving in my desire to know the Lord better. The Word was true honey in my mouth. Serving Jesus in the pulpit and on the streets was the joy of my life.

Then God pulled the world out from under my feet.

Flies in the Ointment

You can't help but wonder why God allows that to happen. Was it all simply because Satan challenged Him?

I think not. While that was the primary cause (and we'll look at that issue in the next chapter), God is not some sadist who allows the testing of His children on a whim. He had far more planned than just proving Satan wrong. In fact, He has assured us in the New Testament that for those who love Him He works everything in their lives for good, even the terrible things. Paul said God is doing this to make us like Jesus, who was perfected through suffering (Romans 8:29; Hebrews 2:10). It's legitimate to assume that there were areas in Job's life that God wanted to eliminate, transform, develop, and stretch. What might they have been?

In this respect, I see three problem areas in Job's life that the Lord might have been working to correct. I don't mean to say these are the primary causes of Job's trial. No one pinned a single sin on Job that warranted judgment. In fact, Job's trial was not a judgment. It was part of God's growth plan for His child.

But when we go through the kind of trial Job did, we must keep before our eyes the fact that God is shaping us into the image of Jesus. No matter how mature Job was, or how much he'd accomplished, God had more planned for him than the keeping of the weekly sacrifices.

It's these aspects of Job's nature that I'm thinking of. God would use this trial not only to prove Satan wrong once for all, but to conform Job a little more to the image of Jesus.

Remember also that these weaknesses only came out in the context of the trial. Often a Christian can appear to "have it all together" on the surface. Like newly mined gold, he can shine rather adequately. But when the fire of testing is applied, all the dross comes to the surface. Even Job said, "When He has tried me, I shall come forth as gold" (23:10). It's only through testing that God is able to expose and eliminate impurities from our lives.

What then were those impurities? I see three.

An Unbalanced View of God's Sovereignty

Though many Christians underemphasize God's power and position in our world, Job did just the opposite. He saw everything as the immediate result of God's actions. We see this initially in his reaction to the disasters that took his livestock, servants, and children. Job tore his robe, shaved his head, fell to the ground, worshiped, and said, "The Lord gave and the Lord has taken away. Blessed be the name of the Lord" (1:21). It's a marvelous statement of faith. Job rightly viewed God as Ruler of the universe, the Giver of all things, the One who blesses, and the One who withholds blessing. This is an absolute. Job knew it and relied upon it.

Even Paul reminded us to think in these terms. He said, "Rejoice in the Lord always" (Philippians 4:4) in a context where he speaks of difficult circumstances. But *notice it's "the Lord" we rejoice in, not the circumstances.* We can rejoice in Him because we know He's in control, that nothing has taken Him by surprise, that it's all part of His plan, that He's moving us toward ultimate glory and victory. Paul also wrote to the Thessalonians, "In everything give thanks" (1 Thessalonians 5:18). How could we give thanks if we didn't believe what was happening was from the hand of a good, loving, wise, and all-powerful Lord?

Even James said, "Consider it all joy, my brethren, when you encounter various trials . . ." (James 1:2–4). Paul echoes the same thought in Romans, "We also exult in our tribulations, knowing that tribulation brings about perseverance . . ." (Romans 5:3). And again Paul asserted, "We know that God causes all things to work together for good . . ." (Romans 8:28). Without a belief in God's absolute sovereignty over all creation these statements make no sense. We rejoice, give thanks, persevere, and stand firm because of *who* God is, not *what we are.*

Yet it's possible to turn God's sovereignty into a monster. Some people move from seeing God in control and God as sovereign to God as *the immediate cause* of everything. They believe everything that happens happens because God makes it happen. They see Him as the master computer operator who pushes a button and Joe Doe dies. He pulls a lever and an earthquake flattens California. He whispers and a tornado rips through Kansas and leaves hundreds homeless and many dead.

Job also saw his disasters as the result of God's actions. For instance, Job says in 9:17–18, "He bruises me with a tempest, and multiplies my wounds without cause. He will not allow me to get my breath, but saturates me with bitterness." Somehow Job imagined that God Himself had turned Job into His personal punching bag. Even in 9:24, Job asks, "If it is not He, then who is it?"

Again in 16:9 Job says, "His anger has torn me and hunted me down, He has gnashed at me with His teeth." Then in verse 11, he goes on, "God hands me over to ruffians, and tosses me into the hands of the wicked. I was at ease, but He shattered me, and He has grasped me by the neck and shaken me to pieces; He has also set me up as His target." It's a graphic image. You can almost see Job splayed out on the bull's eye, while his sadistic father in heaven draws a fiery arrow and shoots off his kneecaps!

But is this an accurate picture? Was God doing this to Job?

We know from the text that *Satan* was the immediate cause of all this trouble. God personally had done nothing but take down the "hedge" He'd put up around Job. But even that hedge was an act of grace. Job hadn't merited it. There was no deal made between God and him that required God to erect it permanently. God could put up the hedge or take it down as He pleased and Job could say nothing.

Furthermore, God didn't force or advise Satan to do anything to Job. He didn't climb down from His throne and say, "Now

Satan, I'd like you to make it rough on him. No easy treatment. Wipe the guy out."

Not at all. In fact, God placed fixed limits on Satan to prevent him from going too far.

If anyone was to be blamed for Job's agonies it was Satan, not the Lord.

Yet I know that when I went through the trials I did, the first thing I said was, "Lord, why are *You* doing this to me?" Most of us tend to have this idea that since God is sovereign, He's supposed to make everything work out perfectly. Nothing is supposed to touch us as long as we're walking with Him.

This is the very problem that leads many Christians to despair when they go through trials. They can't imagine how God could ever let anything bad happen to them. They turn His sovereignty into a magic genie that's supposed to push all problems, trials, difficulties, and irritations away the moment we say "Go!" As a result, when we suddenly find ourselves in the midst of terrible circumstances, we crumble, blame God, and accuse Him of not caring, not being just, not acting in a loving manner, not having our best interests in mind.

We must come back to the truth that while God is in absolute control of all of life, He is not the cause of all life's mishaps. Rather, His plan *allows* those mishaps for the great purpose of raising up "many brethren conformed to the image of Christ" (Romans 8:29).

Job's trial exposed this important misinterpretation on Job's part. God wants us to view Him in all His majesty. But to see God as He is, we must see Him accurately. An unfocused image of God will distort our whole way of dealing with the rest of life.

A Man-Centered View of God's Wisdom

Job's second problem concerned God's wisdom. He couldn't understand how God could allow these things to continue—let alone happen. For instance, he cries in 3:11, "Why did I not die at birth, come forth from the womb and expire?" In other words, "Why did God even let me live beyond birth if He was planning to do this to me?"

Later in the same chapter he asks, "Why is light given to a man whose way is hidden, and whom God has hedged in?" (3:23). Job means, "Why does God let me continue to live if I have to live this way? What's the point? Why doesn't He simply kill me?"

Again, in his second speech, he cries, "What is my strength that I should wait? And what is my end, that I should endure?" (6:11). He's saying, "Does God think I'm made of metal that I can take this kind of punishment forever? At least have Him tell me how long this agony will last. Then I could endure it."

Job's cries are understandable, aren't they? He had no answers. He was slammed into a corner, pummeled featureless, and nearly left for dead. Furthermore, he had no assurance the trial would end soon or otherwise. That's what makes such a trial so difficult—the uncertainty when it will end, the fear that it may never end.

We can all identify with Job. During my depression the problem that terrified me daily was the fear that I would never come out of it, that I was going to be like this for the rest of my life. Each day I couldn't imagine bearing another hour of anguish. The idea of it lasting weeks annihilated my spirit.

At the same time, I couldn't understand how God in His wisdom could allow this. I couldn't see any good coming from this. I was useless for service, inert in faith, haggard in appearance, and despondent in outlook. How could God let this go on?

The reason we see things this way is because we don't understand how God thinks; we can't comprehend the nature of His wisdom. "His thoughts are not our thoughts; His ways are not our ways," said Isaiah (55:8). When we're new in the faith, or immature, we tend to think that God will always do what is best for us. Indeed, He will. But what *we* think is best and what *He* does are as different as whipped cream and concrete. We think He'll make us happy. In effect, we envision these warm, fuzzy feelings. But He plans to make us holy. That often calls for plenty of knocks and raps. We expect that He'll meet our needs. In our minds this means paid bills and something extra for weekends. But His purpose may be to teach us to live within our means, to curtail spending, and become sound stewards of our possessions. That might require teaching us some stiff self-denial and hardheaded planning.

Job's problem was just like ours. We have one plan and God has another. But God's plan is the one that will be put into operation. And when those plans turn into real life circumstances, we can feel as though we've been drawn, quartered, and fed to the crows.

But it's through gaining God's perspective that we begin to see true wisdom. That was what God was bringing Job to understand.

An Inappropriate Expectation that God Owes Us an Explanation

Job's third area of weakness was the human tendency to require an explanation for everything that happens to us. We see him in 6:24 demanding, "Show me how I have erred!" In 7:20–21 he says, "What have I done to Thee . . . ? Why hast Thou set me as Thy target, so that I am a burden to myself? Why then dost Thou not pardon my transgression and take away my iniquity?" He takes up the cry once more in 10:2, "Let me know why Thou dost contend with me." All through the narrative Job challenges, pleads, cries, "Tell me *why* this is happening, God! At least let me know that!"

Without question, this is my greatest trouble in trials. Somehow I feel that if I know *why* something is happening I can bear it. I also tend to think that if I can find out why it's happened, I'll also discover the solution to the problem.

But is it that simple? Does merely knowing why a problem exists offer real comfort? In fact, in Job's case, his discovery of why—in terms of the challenge voiced by Satan—could actually have led to great problems and questions, even to serious doubt about God's character.

Similarly, knowing why cancer has infected our bodies ("Your diet wasn't right") or the reason a child was killed in traffic ("The driver was drunk") doesn't solve anything. It only raises further questions. "How could You do this, God? Why didn't You stop me (or them)? What kind of person are You to let this happen?"

Furthermore, could God ever offer a satisfactory explanation to Job? For instance, imagine Job's conversation with the Lord in this situation.

"Lord, these boils are awful. Would You mind telling me why this has happened?"

"Not at all. Which explanation do you want—the biological, chemical, historical, moral, spiritual, demonic, divine, or eternal one?"

"Hmm. Well, let's start with the biological one."

"Certainly. Your boils were caused by an outbreak of a certain bacterium, spleenogogus, which normally would have died upon impact with your skin, but at the time your mouth was open (you were eating a bit of asparagus) and it blew right down your throat. Of course, ordinarily it would have been killed by the digestive juices, but because of a certain Vitamin B12 Complex deficiency, it survived, underwent mitosis, multiplied, and spread. This particular bacterium was carried by a crow, on feather number 4,792, where it was able to cultivate a certain biochemical resistance to . . ."

"Wait, wait. Okay, I get the picture. Let's move on to the historical explanation."

"Should I begin with the sin of Adam and Eve in the garden and work My way forward, or would you like Me to start with this moment and go backward outlining the precise factors that led to this circumstance?"

"Uh, why don't we move on to the demonic explanation?"

"Should I begin with Satan's request, or before?"

"Uh, yes. Well how about Satan's request?"

"In that respect, Satan asked that I let down your hedge so he could afflict you and prove that you would curse Me to My face, thereby proving once and for all that all humans are selfishly motivated and serve me only for what they get."

"You mean Satan's the cause of all this trouble!?"

"Well, not exactly, as I said there is a biological, chemical, . . ."

"Yes, yes, I see. But why did Satan want to destroy me?"

"Put most simply, it's because he's evil."

"Now that's something that's always troubled me, Lord. Why precisely is Satan so evil, Lord? I thought he was once the highest archangel, perfect in every way?"

"You're correct. But he became evil."

"But if he was perfect, Lord, how could he go bad?"

"It happens."

"It happens! You mean all You have to say about the one who has messed up everything in history is that it happens?!"

"Which explanation do you want, the Creator-creature argument for risking everything, the free agent proof from original Law, the genuine love or nothing analysis, the . . ."

"Hold it! Hold it! Look, Lord, this is getting difficult. Isn't there something simpler, something I could grasp?"

"Well, yes, there is."

"What's that?"

"Let Me keep it all worked out and you simply trust Me about it."

"Hmmm."

You can see the problem. When we begin demanding explanations for this problem and that crisis, we're bucking up against omniscience. There is no simple line-by-line explanation. A thousand variables are involved. It's much easier simply to pull back and look to Him, to put our faith in His Word, to rely on His promises that say, "I will never leave you or forsake you" and "I will make all things work together for good." If we scream for a computer printout with all the details we may suddenly find ourselves in a billion volume library! And that's just the explanation for the boils!

So Much More To It
But these thoughts are minor compared to the idea that God put Job into Satan's hands. While the Lord might have desired to scour away a few blemishes from Job's theology, that single fact—that Satan came to God, taunted Him about Job's loyalty, and God gave him license to attack—makes everything else

appear ludicrous. God could have dealt with Job's imperfections without resorting to this, couldn't He? We'll discuss that in the next chapter.

Things to Think About or Discuss:
1. Try to picture Job in a modern context. What does he look like? What kind of work does he do? What's he like in the church?
2. What qualities that Job possessed do you see in yourself that you value? Describe them. Why are these important to you? Why do you think God considers them important?
3. How legitimate do you think it is to talk about Job as having certain deficiencies that God wanted to deal with? Why would God choose such a trial to deal with those problems? In light of Job and the areas the chapter raised, what areas of weakness do you see in yourself?
4. When you go through troubles, do you usually seek an explanation? Why or why not? What kinds of answers have you gotten? Did they satisfy you?

3
God Gives Satan a Chance

*H*arold Kushner, a Jewish Rabbi, recently wrote a bestseller called *Why Bad Things Happen to Good People.* After much discussion and illustration, he reaches the conclusion that bad things happen to good people because we live in an imperfect world. While God loves us and cares about our plight, He cannot do much to prevent mishap in our lives. He's as strapped as we are. The best we can hope for is that He sympathizes and understands.

Strangely, the author offers little comment on the scenes played out in the first two chapters of Job. If he had, he might have reached different conclusions. For the first two chapters reveal precisely why Job suffered as he did: Satan attacked him.

Still, that attitude is really not so strange. Few people today give much credence to a belief in Satan and the powers of darkness. Those who do often give him more than he deserves ("It looks like he's winning!" or "The devil made me do it!"). Or they'll give him less ("If Satan exists at all, he's certainly not paying much attention to us").

C.S. Lewis pointed out in *The Screwtape Letters* that these are precisely the two extremes to avoid in thinking about Satan. The truth is that he does exist and he can afflict people and influence our world, but he's as much subject to God's laws as the rest of us. He's not free to roam about and knock down whomever he pleases.

Striking Fear in the Heart of Man

Any thinking Christian who tangles with the Book of Job will discover one of the most amazing facts in Scripture: Satan requested to attack Job and God let him! This raises more questions than any could answer. Furthermore, we have to wonder —could this happen to me? Would God allow Satan to strike me down? Indeed, the first two chapters of Job prickles my skin.

But before we can really tackle the issue of God vanishing, we must ask: How could God put Job into Satan's hands like that? What was His purpose? Is this some cosmic whim, or worse, a divine joke? If so, our God is not much better than the devil himself and deserves our utmost malice and rejection. So what was really happening in this incredible story?

Angels and Devils Reporting In, Sir!

In Job 1:6, the author says that "there was a day when the sons of God came to present themselves before the Lord." The "sons of God" is a reference to God's angels. Apparently, all the angels of God report in now and then to inform Him of their activities. The Hebrew word for "present" means to "station yourself before someone" to await orders. It's like when the colonels meet with the general to discuss tactics and receive their final directions.

One of angels present was Satan, which means "accuser." He is the once regal but now fallen archangel Lucifer (meaning "shining one") who rebelled against God, sought to pull off a coup, and failed. But in the process, he persuaded one-third of the other angels to come along with him. He's their commanding officer and has them organized in ranks much like an army. He's shrewd—the smartest being God ever created; handsome—His most beautiful creation; and sinister—a liar to the core.

God asks Satan what he's been doing. Satan replies rather flippantly, "From roaming about on the earth and walking around on it" (1:7). Notice his lack of specificity and the insolence of the statement. It's as though Satan has to give his report so he decides to avoid it by saying, "What's it to You, God? I've been doing my thing, like I always do! If You want more details, You'll have to press me about it." Always the cocky child.

But as always, God stays calm and asks if during his travels he's crossed paths with Job. God's interested particularly in certain facets of Job's character—namely the fact that "There is no one like him on earth, a blameless and upright man, fearing God and turning away from evil" (1:8). God not only wants to know what Satan thinks of Job, He's interested to find out his thinking on why Job is so loyal and obedient to Him. This is a critical issue and we have to understand why God asks it.

To answer, I'm going to take a leap onto some rather rough soil. It concerns my whole understanding of the rebellion of Lucifer and the fall of man. Paul told the Ephesians that one reason for the church's existence was "in order that the manifold wisdom of God might now be made known through the church to the rulers and authorities in the heavenly places" (Ephesians 3:1). I believe *one* reason (not the only reason or even the primary reason) that God created the universe, humanity, and the plan of redemption through faith in Christ was to offer the angels an object lesson which He would use to portray His true character.

Remember that because of Satan, God has a rebellion on His hands. One-third of the angels oppose him. While the other two-thirds remain loyal, they probably have a multitude of questions. There was only one way for the Lord to regain their complete loyalty and love and prove once and for all the injustice of Satan's insubordination: through a visible demonstration of His worth. The result? The universe and the ultimate salvation of man through Jesus Christ. (Of course, this is not, as I said, the only reason. But I believe it's one.) This would once and for all prove His "manifold wisdom" (Ephesians 3:1)—it would show the true breadth and depth of His ability to lead, think, rule, and do what's best for all.

Satan's Conviction

Still, we have to ask what led Satan to rebel and how he convinced others to do so. From Isaiah 14:12–14 and Ezekiel 28:11–19 we see why he rebelled: he wanted God's place. He wasn't content to be a servant and worshiper of God. He wanted the worship for himself. He was proud and jealous.

But he couldn't tell all the other angels this. Even though Satan was wiser than them, more striking, powerful, and awesome, angels are intelligent beings. They would see right through his motives. What then might Satan have promised them if they would join his side? Probably the same things crooks promise their followers: a piece of the action, a high position, the spoils, etc. So they joined him. Satan, being a wise and incredibly powerful presence, persuaded them to fight God. Undoubtedly these other angels had similar aspirations to Satan. They wanted to be God.

Nonetheless, the rebellion failed. God stopped the demonic hordes and proved Himself more powerful than Satan.

So what happened then? Satan had to prove God was wrong, that He was a fraud, that He was unworthy, that He couldn't lead, and that no one should follow Him.

So what did Satan do? After leading Adam and Eve into sin, he worked up a theory. It's this: since God isn't really worthy of our love and worship, there is only one reason anyone ever loves and obeys Him—because of what He gives them. He was saying, in effect, that no person ever follows God because of *who* He is. People (and angels) only fear Him because of *what* they get out of Him or what He will do to them if they don't. If Satan can prove this, he can topple the whole kingdom, for then no one will ever really love God. They either obey Him out of stark terror or because they want something from Him, like fawning teacher's pets. In effect, Satan would achieve the ruin of everything the Lord had done. They'd all end up cursing God to His face. *And* following the person who would give them more!

Never Convinced

Now we can see why God points out Job to Satan. Job proves Satan's theory is bunk. He's one more example that Satan speaks nothing but lies.

Just the same, Satan's not convinced. He retorts, "Does Job fear God for nothing? Hast Thou not made a hedge about him and his house and all that he has, on every side? Thou hast blessed the work of his hands, and his possessions have increased in the land. But put forth Thy hand now and touch all that he has; and he will surely curse Thee to Thy face!" (1:9–11).

What an illuminating picture of Satan's character. This statement reveals all. First, his complaint unveils his pet theory: no one loves and fears God because He is worthy. They only fear Him for what He does for them. Satan is really saying, "Job only fears You because You've blessed him so much. It means nothing. If he didn't have all that stuff You give him, he'd be off in a flash."

Second, Satan's frustrated. He couldn't touch Job! In fact, no one could touch Job! God had placed a "hedge" about him. For years, Satan wanted to destroy Job (because he contradicted his theory). He'd lusted after Job's destruction—because he loathes anyone who loves God. But God put up His protective shield and Satan was powerless to knock it down.

Isn't that incredible? In fact, Scripture reveals in several places that we all have the same hedge about us. John wrote in 1 John 5:18, "He (Christ) who was born of God keeps him and the evil one does not touch him." When Jesus told Satan to leave during the temptation in the wilderness (Matthew 4:10–11), Satan had to go. Similarly, we see Jesus repeatedly casting out demons who were powerless to remain when He gave a command. Finally, when Peter told Jesus he would never deny Him, Jesus told him that Satan had *"demanded permission* to sift him like wheat" (Luke 22:31). Satan couldn't do a thing to Peter unless God allowed it!

That's a wonderful truth because I've known many Christians (including myself) who lived in steady terror of the powers of darkness. But Satan's complaint demonstrates once again that he's nothing. One whiff from God and he gets blown right out of the stadium!

Third, it shows Satan's rage about all this. Job is stealing his limelight. Angels are rejecting his theory. Perhaps some even regret that they followed him. Every time any Christian seeks to glorify God because He's worthy, Satan's malice goes up to ten on the Richter scale. He doesn't like to be proved wrong.

Thus, Satan drops his gauntlet. "Put forth Thy hand now and touch all that he has; he will surely curse Thee to Thy face" (1:11). In other words, "God, find out for Yourself why Job obeys You. You're deluded. You sit up there on Your throne, but You don't know reality. Everyone thinks You and Your kingdom are a bale of baloney!"

The Most Amazing Fact of All

At this point, I suspect that the whole gathering of angels are on the edge of their wing tips! Some are ready to cheer, "Yeah, God, let's see what happens. Let's see if Job sticks with You after everything's taken away. Wipe him out." Other angels are afraid. "Boy, what if this falls through, Lord? You could look pretty bad." But the challenge has been laid. Can God walk away from it?

Let's face it. God could turn around and say, "Satan, you're impudent. Get out of My sight." But what happens then? Everyone becomes skeptical. And God never operates in an atmosphere of doubt and fear. He has nothing to hide. He can meet any challenge in the light of day.

So what does He do? To me, it's the most startling response in all of Scripture. He gives Satan a chance to attack Job!

But take note. What had Satan requested? "*You* touch all he has, God, and he'll curse You to Your face." But God could never commit an evil act against anyone. God deftly places any blame for evil at Satan's feet.

We must realize that God isn't *using* Satan to get His ends done. He didn't cause Satan to do anything to Job. As I said before, all He did was take down Job's hedge. God never promised to keep Job from having problems, nor did He promise always to keep things going well. He hasn't even promised us those things. The hedge around Job was an act of grace, not a contractual agreement. So He could put it up or take it down as He desired.

Furthermore, God never counseled Satan to commit an iota of sin. Satan was wholly responsible for any and every crime.

So God says, "Behold, all that he has is in *your* power, only do not put forth your hand on him" (1:12). If Satan wanted to harm Job, that was Satan's responsibility. God would have nothing to do with it.

Still, notice again that God even placed limits on Satan—another act of grace. Satan couldn't hurt Job, only his possessions.

Nonetheless, we're a bit shocked. How can God do this—put a living, throbbing, pain-feeling human being into the hands of Satan just to prove to Satan he's wrong? Isn't this the ultimate paradox of the book—God trying to prove Satan's wrong at Job's expense?

The Critical Issue

This will continue to mystify us if we don't think it through. Furthermore, it could make us think God is unjust. But we gain a glimmer of insight through a special Greek term, which we translate in different contexts by our words, "test" and "tempt."

This word is from the Greek root, *PEIRADZO*. Matthew used it when he said, "Jesus was led up by the Spirit into the wilderness to be *tempted* by the devil" (Matthew 4:1). James used it in James 1:2: "Consider it all joy when you encounter various *trials*, knowing that the testing of your faith produces endurance." Obviously, God allows such trials and temptations for a purpose.

Yet the same word is used in James 1:13 in a wholly different way. James says here, "Let no one say when he is *tempted*, 'I am being *tempted* by God,' for God cannot be *tempted* by evil, and He Himself does not *tempt* anyone." How can God let Jesus be led by the Spirit to be tempted by the devil, yet James says God never tempts anyone? The same Greek root is used in all cases.

The problem is in the English meaning of the word, *temptation.* To "tempt" in English means "to entice someone to evil." In fact, that is precisely Satan's purpose to entice us to do wrong. But the Greek word carried a double-edged meaning. The positive aspect of temptation was "testing." A *test* was meant to show that something or someone was good and right!

Consider an example. Imagine that you're a new Ford Mustang just off the production line. Also imagine that there are two test drivers for this car, God and Satan. Now what's Satan's purpose? He wants to show that the car—you—can't perform at all. He wants to demonstrate that you're fallible, that you're bogus stuff, not worth the expense and not up to even the simplest performance standards.

God, on the other hand, has a different purpose. He wants to show what that car can do—how well it hugs the road, speeds up, slows down, uses gas economically. He wants to prove it's a fine machine adequate to every command. Or He may be seeking to perfect the car through revealing its weaknesses. Whichever, His purpose is admirable and righteous.

As a result, in any test/temptation, while God wants to show how good we are or where the bugs are, Satan wants to prove what goofs we are! Thus, the same test has diverging purposes from the standpoint of the testers.

The Ultimate Test of Faith
Still we have to ask why this is necessary. We can see the point with Ford Mustangs or Anacin or Pepsi Cola, but why do this to Job? Just to prove a point?

Yes! And what a point—the most important point in all of creation. For what is the test about? It's this: will a person love and obey God even when all the goodies are taken away? That is the critical test not only of all of history, but also for each one of us. Will we go God's way and keep on loving Him even when there's nothing immediately in it for us?

Do you see the cruciality of such a test? If Job, Jesus, Peter, and everyone else including us serve God just because He's given us heaven, salvation, eternal life, and abundant joy, love, and peace, it ultimately comes down to selfishness. We're only in it for what we get. In fact, that's the big come-on many evangelists use to get people to come to Christ. "Trust Jesus and God'll give you . . ." The list of goodies goes on forever. Christianity—faith—becomes little more than an exercise in the gimmes.

Moreover, that is exactly what Satan believes and would have us believe: that God is little more than a Super Duper Supermarket dispensing bribes to His "saints." Therefore, He's not really worthy of genuine love, loyalty, worship, and devotion. So Satan says, "Come, follow me, and I'll give you better things than God ever could."

This is always Satan's tactic—promise them more than they think God will give, and in their selfishness, they'll go your way. This was what he did with Eve—"God knows that in the day you eat of it (the forbidden fruit), you'll be like God" (which appeared to be more than God was willing to give, although she was already like God, being in His image). He did that with Jesus—"All this will I give you (the kingdoms of the world), if you fall down and worship me." Satan always promises to give us things that he says God won't give us Himself—pleasure, power, wealth, honor!

As a result, this is a test we all must pass. That's why God allows us to go through the "troughs" when he seems far away, as Lewis said, and through trials, sufferings, and periods when He seems to vanish. Suddenly, all the props are taken away. No more fuzzy feelings. Life is tough. Pain breaks our consciousness every waking hour. We cry, "What are You doing, God? Why aren't You blessing me?" Suddenly, we find out which we really love—Him or His blessings.

For such a trial, God knows precisely what He must take away in order to prove our faith is the real thing. For each of us it's different. For some it's health. For others, it's money. For others, it's a good emotional life, or a career, or a prize, or something else. But when He lets Satan snatch those riches away, our true heart shows. It's then that He asks, "Now that you have nothing left but Me, do you still love *Me?* Will you still obey *Me?*"

Think about it. Don't you long to be loved because of *who you are*—not what you do or give? That is the essence of love. God wants us to love Him because He's worthy and loving Him is right. He wants us to love other people because they're made in His image. He wants us to choose to love freely—a love that's not conditional on performance, gifts, kindnesses, or other deeds. He wants us to love because it's right, good, holy, and Godlike to love. Nothing the loved one does can change our decision to love him.

Can you imagine that—a whole universe populated by people who choose to love on that basis? That's exactly where God's taking us—to such a place! One day, all people from all time who have believed, obeyed, and loved God because He alone is worthy will gather together in one place forever. I for one can't even begin to imagine how fantastic the worship, kindness, generosity, and general goodwill would be in such a place. But I long for it. Don't you?

Your Test

This is why I believe God must allow us all to undergo such a test. He must demonstrate to the world, the angels, and the powers of darkness that we love Him for the right reasons. It's the essence of faith in Christ. That's why Jesus said, "He who does not take up his cross and follow after Me is not worthy of Me" (Matthew 10:38).

So ask yourself, "Why am I a Christian? Why do I go to church? Why do I follow Christ?"

Is it because Jesus makes you feel good, because He got your finances straightened out, because He fixed up your marriage? Those are decent reasons, but ultimately they're not enough. What happens when you don't feel good, or the money goes, or your marriage sails through the rocks?

On both the first and last lines of all of our statements of faith, there must be one personal decree: "Lord, I choose to love, obey, follow, and worship You because You alone *are* worthy."

That's what Job is all about. That's what your life now is all about. It's the final test of faith. My prayer is that both you and I will pass.

Things to Think About or Discuss:

1. How does the story in Job 1 and 2 strike you? What reasons do you think God might have had in letting Satan attack Job?

2. How do you think Satan feels about you? Would he desire to attack you? Why or why not?

3. We discussed at length Satan's conviction that all people are out to get what they can for themselves. Do you think this is legitimate? Why or why not?

4. Do you think it's necessary for God to prove that your faith is real and to find out the reasons you serve Him? Why do you serve Him? What are your strongest reasons?

4
When You Feel There's No Hope Left

So God put Job into Satan's hands.

That's scary enough. Even though we can understand God's reasoning here to some degree, it looks rather hopeless. Kind of like placing a baby in a lion's den and telling the lions, "You can do anything to her except eat her." Everyone looks on in terror wondering if the lions will obey.

In this case, however, we're dealing with supernatural forces which are mystifying. Our world churns with fear of the supernatural. Stephen King has made a fortune chilling the spines of people who flock to the bookstores and movie houses to see what new terror his mind has unleashed into our imaginations. We tend to think that such things are absolutely uncontrollable, which is a part of their power over us. But is the world of the supernatural uncontrollable? Is Satan, who prowls about like a roaring lion, able to sink his teeth into anyone at his leisure or pleasure?

Would God Put Us Into Satan's Hands?
This is where the Book of Job offers incredible hope to all of us. Would God ever put us into the hands of Satan like He did with Job?

Possibly, but it really doesn't matter. Job serves as the prototype of all such tests. He's like the marathoner who went the full 26 miles, 385 yards. God let Satan take Job to the limits of human endurance to prove once and for all that His children will stand by Him even when every blessing is sheared away. Job was the first and final proof that a man will remain loyal to God even when God ceases to bless him.

But on the other hand, all of us must stand the test—will we stick with God even when we have nothing left in this world but Him? We must burn in that crucible under God's conditions for the sake of our testimony, our endurance, and our unquestioned allegiance to Him throughout all eternity. Therefore we can expect that God will test us in this way. Study any figure in biblical history and you will find God took him through such rigors to prove his faith—Abraham, Daniel, Shadrach, Meshach, and Abednego, the disciples, and even Jesus are some good examples.

Job in the Midst of It
Job remained steadfast and immovable at the beginning of his trial. He didn't know why such calamities were happening to him. But he remained faithful. He continued to worship God. The author said, "In all this Job did not sin with his lips" (2:10). Even when his wife told him to "curse God and die"—to tell God he wanted nothing ever to do with Him again, and then kill himself (perhaps as a last act of revenge on Him)—Job didn't flinch or quiver. He was loyal to his Lord.

But as time advanced and Job's condition worsened, he strangled on those questions and feelings that march with hobnailed boots upon our souls. His body was covered with sore boils—running wounds (2:7). His skin itched so horribly that he began scratching himself with the piece of a broken pottery (2:8). He sat in a pile of ashes (indicating his mourning). His pain was so acute that his three friends said nothing to him for seven days. They simply sat and grieved with him (2:13).

In addition, worms writhed among his sores, now covered with dirt because washing himself was too painful (7:5). His skin became brittle and ran with ooze, while his bones flamed within him like ovens (3:3). When he tried to sleep, vivid nightmares pummeled his mind till he awoke screaming (7:14). He lost weight and sleep (16:7–8) and wept so much his body's fluids dried up. Toward the end of his misery, he lost so much weight that his bones clung to his flesh (19:20). He became utterly exhausted, unable to relax or rest even for a moment (30:27). In his niche in the wilderness, jackals came by to watch, presumably to wait for him to die so they might eat his flesh (30:29).

What incredible pain! How could he endure it?

What Job Didn't Know

What Job didn't know at the time, and which we do know, are several important truths about the nature of such a test. We could easily think that if God puts us into Satan's hands all is lost. But our Lord is not some Nazi bent on performing wrenching experiments to test the endurance of people. Rather He set some severe and restricting limits on Satan that offer us great hope in the midst of our trials. What are those limits? And how do they offer hope?

The Hedge

The first thing we notice when we plunge into Job is that Satan was enraged and frustrated. Why? Because God had put a "hedge" around Job.

The Hebrew word used here means a protective fence through which no one could pass. Solomon used the word in Proverbs 15:19 when he said, "The way of the sluggard is as a hedge of thorns, but the path of the upright is a highway." Such a hedge prevents progress. You're constantly fighting to make headway, and ultimately you give up.

Hosea also prophesied concerning his errant wife Gomer that he would put a hedge of thorns around her and "build a wall against her" so that she couldn't continue to commit adultery.

Have you ever run up against such a hedge? One of our neighbors had one when I was a child. It was a high, thorny, thick line of bushes that lined their yard. I once found a small dog caught in it. He had tried to wriggle under, but the sharp thorns were so painful he ended up stuck, unable to go back or forward. On another occasion, I was being chased by some local bullies and ran into their yard by a secret way. The bullies were on one side and I on the other. They rattled the branches, shouted threats, and even beat at the hedge with sticks. But I knew they couldn't get through. I even began taunting them, and then I hightailed it for home.

Satan's complaint was that God had constructed just such a hedge about Job and all he had. Satan couldn't touch Job.

That's a startling truth, because most of us think of Satan as invincible. When I first became a Christian I was so frightened of Satan that I slept with a Bible under my pillow for several weeks. In another instance, I visited a doctor who was also a Christian. While I tried to share my testimony with him, his phone kept ringing. He said, "Satan's trying to keep us from talking." (I thought it was because people were sick!) Even Paul told the Thessalonians that he'd tried to come to them several times, but "Satan thwarted him" (1 Thessalonians 2:18).

Nonetheless, Satan possesses no power to touch any Christian apart from God's will. When Peter assured Jesus he'd not only fight for Him but die for Him, Jesus replied, "Simon, Simon, behold, Satan has demanded permission to sift you like wheat . . ." (Luke 22:31).

Notice that Satan had to "demand permission." He couldn't simply sashay over to Peter's house and unleash a thunderbolt on him; he had to ask God's permission. In fact, the text intimates that Satan had to "demand" permission. That meant pleading, threatening, finagling, goading, and finally saying he wouldn't have it any other way. He had to throw a fit to get his request. And God only gave it to him for certain distinct eternal purposes, not on a whim. God never grants such permissions lightly.

John also tells us that "the whole world lies in the power of the evil one" (1 John 5:19). Nonetheless, Satan has no power to touch those who belong to Christ (1 John 5:18) because Christ Himself keeps Satan away from us.

This truth provides awe-inspiring hope to anyone who has known the fear of the darkness. Satan cannot touch us apart from God's will. We're always in the hands of the infinitely loving, perfectly loyal, always purposeful, constantly caring and compassionate Lord of creation. Frankly, I'd rather be in His hands than anyone else's, including my own.

Limits

But this isn't all Job reveals. Not only could Satan not touch Job apart from God's permission, but Satan was also limited by God's decree. Two times God granted to Satan the right to attack Job. The first time he could waylay anything that belonged to Job, but he couldn't attack Job personally (Job 1:12). The second time, God gave him power to strike Job's body, but he couldn't kill him (2:6). With a simple word, Satan was rendered impotent. He could do nothing beyond what God allowed.

This is amazing. How is it that God could issue a simple command and Satan was eternally bound?

One reason: because the word of God—uttered from His lips—is powerful. Whether it's the Scriptures or something like this in which an obvious verbal command is issued, that's all it takes.

Peter himself, who knew Satan's attack power, reminds us of this. He says to those who think that God will never destroy the heavens and earth, or render judgment, "For when they maintain this, it escapes their notice that by the word of the Lord the heavens existed long ago, and the earth was formed out of water and by water . . ." (2 Peter 3:5). God created simply by uttering a command. If He's that powerful, is it not conceivable that His creatures are held by a command? "By faith we understand that the worlds were created by the word of God, so that what is seen was not made out of things which are visible" (Hebrews 11:3).

Peter goes on to say, "But the present heavens and earth by

His word are being reserved for fire . . ." (2 Peter 3:7). Again we see that the only reason the heaven and earth persist are because God commands it.

When God chooses to move against Satan, he will be powerless to resist (Revelation 20:1–4). God casts him into the bottomless pit, binds him there with a chain, and no one makes a peep. The one who strode through the earth like a giant is cut down with a mere word from God!

Again, this is tremendous hope to us who endure the attacks and temptations of the devil. God will not "allow us to be tempted beyond what we are able"; rather He'll "provide a way of escape that we may be able to endure it" (1 Corinthians 10:13). Nothing stymies, stumps, overwhelms, or frazzles Him. He's in perfect control.

One of my favorite Psalms is Psalm 2. Here the leaders of the earth, the great kings, potentates, presidents, and tyrants all gather together, saying, "Let's get rid of God and His Son. They're a real block to our plans." They arm themselves, poise their ballistic missiles, assemble their armies. The great juggernaut moves forward, fists flailing the air before God, saying, "We shall overcome."

What does God do? The psalmist says He sits up in heaven and laughs. He mocks them. "You've got to be kidding," God says. "You think you can beat Me?" Then He speaks in His anger, and suddenly His Son is installed on the hill of Zion, ruling the whole earth with a rod of iron.

Another potent word is found in Isaiah 4:12-31. Isaiah seeks to comfort the beleaguered captives of Israel after they've been deported to Babylon. To remind them of God's greatness and power, Isaiah waxes most eloquently in his graphic depiction of God. He says (my paraphrase):

Who takes up the Atlantic Ocean in the depression of His palm? Who marks off the distance between earth and Orion by stretching out His pinky and thumb? Who puts the mountains on His bathroom floor scale to see how much they weigh? God Almighty! Take a look around you. Russia is a mere drop in a bucket! To Him the United States is like a speck of dust. He could lift up Australia and flick it off His fingertip. He's the one who chooses who rules and who doesn't. God merely blows on Planet Earth and it whisks away into the galaxies. Tell me, can you count the stars? But God has a name for each one. He knows each one personally. How can anyone say, "God doesn't know about me; He doesn't care?" Don't you know? Haven't you heard? The God who lives forever, the Lord and Creator of everything, never gets tired. His wisdom and power to understand is beyond any of us. He is the one who strengthens the weak kneed. He's the one who raises the slumped shoulders. Even though an Olympic decathlon champion stumbles and falls in the race, yet anyone who trusts in and waits on God will have new strength every moment. He'll fly like an eagle. He'll run and never stop. He'll walk, but he'll never have to breathe hard.

Do you get the picture? Anyone on God's side is on the winning team. Satan can't knock him over, spin him around, or shoot him down unless in His perfect wisdom God chooses to allow it for the sake of His perfect plan.

I'm often astounded at the way these truths become a reality despite the onslaughts of Satan. I think of Martin Luther standing before the Diet of Worms and saying he wouldn't recant, even if they burned him at the stake. I think of Jim Elliott going to the murderous Auca Indians, saying, "He is no fool who gives what he cannot keep to gain what he cannot lose." Some have even read the story of Stan Dale in *Lords of the Earth* in which he confronted the errant warriors of Irian Jaya until they began shooting him with arrows. Stan merely broke the arrows off as they struck his own body and pleaded with them to repent. Some fifty arrows struck him before he fell. But the whole village was converted through his witness.

When John Livingstone was traveling in Africa through treacherous territory, a hostile chief had warned him he would be killed. One night Livingstone was so full of fear he opened his Bible and began to read. He came to the text that says, "I am with you always, even to the end of the age" (Matthew 28:20). Suddenly the lights went on in his head. He wrote himself a note that God's promise was the word of a gentleman and therefore could be completely trusted.

The next morning he was warned by his workmen that the chief and his warriors were hiding in the bushes waiting to put an arrow in his back. Livingstone supervised the loading of all the canoes. When all had gone except the last and everyone was in the canoes except him, Livingstone stood a moment on the shore with his back turned to the chief. If the chief wanted to strike him down, that was his chance. But he didn't. God didn't let him. Livingstone had the word of a gentleman of the greatest power and he knew he could trust it. God's power is greater than anything Satan can imagine, muster, or plan.

Endurance

Yet even this is small comfort next to a third fact we find in Job. You see it in Job 2:1 where the author says, "In all this Job did not sin with his lips." Satan's taunt had been that Job, were he to lose all his possessions and even his health, would curse God to his face. But Satan's boast crashed to the ground. Job didn't curse God. Job remained loyal, even though everything in his world had crumbled.

Why didn't Job curse God? Simply because he was strong in faith, unwavering, and better than other men?

No. We all know we're weak. None of us can stand apart from God. "Let him who thinks he stands take heed lest he fall" (1 Corinthians 10:12). "Apart from Me, you can do nothing," Jesus warned the disciples.

Why then did Job remain steadfast? Because God planned it that way. God wasn't going to allow him to give in.

Probably the greatest and most important principle for all of us as Christians is this: every true Christian will persevere to the end of this life because God has planned to enable him to persevere.

It's sometimes called the doctrine of the "perseverance of the saints." It means that all real Christians (there are many fakes, you know) remain loyal and faithful to the Lord no matter how great the trials of this life.

The counterpart to this doctrine is sometimes called *eternal security:* "once saved, always saved." God will not allow any of His children to fall or slide away. If you're truly redeemed, you'll stay redeemed. You can never lose your salvation.

This does not mean there won't be other sorts of casualties. Jesus spoke of several different types of soil on which the gospel is sown. There is the seed sown on the side of the road. They are people who hear the word, but never understand because Satan blinds their eyes and they submit to his blindness. Then there are the seeds sown on the shallow soil. These are so-called believers who hear the word and initially rejoice. But when things get tough, trials come, and persecution and reproaches follow, this person dumps his faith. "It's too hard," he says. The third soil also receives the seed with joy, but once it sprouts, the weeds of materialism, love of money, and the lures of this world choke out the life. This person never reckons with the commandment to take up the cross and follow Christ. He has one foot in the world, and one in religion. He ends up being lost.

But the true Christian bears fruit—spiritual character, the leading of others to Christ, and right conduct—all the days of his life.

We can't make the mistake of thinking that because a person professes to be a Christian that he's automatically saved. The Word tells us repeatedly that there are deceivers, false prophets, wolves in sheep's clothing, heretics, fakes, frauds, and every other sort of pretender imaginable in this world trying to lead us astray. A person may not even know he's false. But the true Christian goes on bearing fruit constantly.

Again, that doesn't mean there won't be times when true Christians fall. David committed adultery and murder. Peter denied the Lord three times, and later went back to the Jewish law for a period of time. Timothy gave up and Paul had to write a whole letter to get him back in an unashamed walk with Jesus. Mark was such a problem for Paul and Barnabas that they split over whether to retain him as a disciple. But in all these cases,

God was faithful. He saw them through despite their sin.

That's what happened with Job. God knew from the beginning that Job would pass the test with Satan. Why? Not only because God is omniscient, but because God *planned* that he pass. As Paul says in Philippians 1:6, "I am confident of this very thing, that He who began a good work in you will perfect it until the day of Christ Jesus." And 1 Corinthians 1:8, He "shall also confirm you to the end, blameless in the day of our Lord Jesus Christ." Even when we're faithless, God remains faithful, Paul reminded Timothy (2 Timothy 2:13). And Jude promised the readers of his letter, "Now to Him who is able to keep you from stumbling, and to make you stand in the presence of His glory, blameless with great joy . . ." (v. 24). God's plan is to get us all on the way to glory, no matter how much Satan and everyone else may be opposed to it.

That's a remarkable piece of hope, isn't it? God plans that we pass the tests of faith of this life, even though there may be setbacks on the way. He wants to display us before the hosts of heaven as examples of His goodness and glory.

I remember when this truth first hit home to me. I was working on a beach project in Wildwood, New Jersey. Someone had told me that I could lose my salvation if I wasn't careful. He said, "It's like shaking hands with someone. You put out your hand and God puts out his. If we let go, we lose our salvation."

I was terrified because I knew if anyone could lose it I would. I lost my first watch in seventh grade. I lost my first girlfriend in twelfth. I almost didn't make it through college. And seminary was hard as nails. I knew that if you could lose it, I may as well give up right then and there and not even try, because sooner or later it would creep up on me, pounce, and I'd be on hell's soon-to-arrive list.

But that summer I happened to be working with several young theologians from Westminster Seminary. They worked through a lot of Scripture with me. One day a friend gave me this illustration (after I'd told him about the one above with the shaking hands). He said, "Mark, did you ever go out for a walk with your dad when you were little and there was snow on the ground?"

"Sure."

"Did he hold your hand?"

"Of course."

"His hand was bigger than yours, right?"

"Yup."

"Did you ever slip?"

"Of course."

"What happened?"

"My feet went out from under me, my whole body shot out, and Dad's hand gripped mine and held me up until I got my balance."

Then he said, "Let me show you a verse in Psalm 37." He read from verses 23 and 24: "The steps of a man are established by the Lord; and He delights in his way. When he falls, he shall not be hurled headlong; because the Lord is the one who holds his hand."

Instantly I had the picture. The only way we could shake hands and let go is if God is equal to us in strength. But God is much greater—so much greater that His hand could fit the whole Atlantic Ocean in its palm. Do you think any of us could ever slip out of that grip?

When I was stumbling along during the days of my depression, thinking at any moment I would commit suicide or act in a sinful way, I kept coming back to this truth. Often I prayed, "Lord, please don't let me go. I'm going to give up on my own. But I trust You not to allow that to happen."

Through two and a half years I gave up daily. But each day the Lord brought experiences, encouragements, and little victories that made me realize He was with me.

On one occasion I was so depressed I couldn't complete a term paper. As I trudged down the street to my job hoping to complete the paper that night, I spotted a little robin in a bird's nest. It was winter. Snow was on the ground. A fierce wind was whipping the naked trees about me. And here was this robin, sitting in its nest on its eggs. "Nuts!" I said. "Crazy!" Then I looked a little closer. The robin had its eyes closed, its face was turned into the wind, it had nestled deeper down in its nest, and its topmost head feathers were parted neatly. At the same time, the whole tree was pitching about, ready to cast that bird and its nest into oblivion.

But it wasn't cast off. The bird seemed to have no concern that it could catapult into oblivion, only that it hang in there till the end of the storm.

I walked away smiling. I felt as though God had given me a special message. "Hang in there, Mark. I'm with you."

What Job Found Out

What Job was also discovering was that God was holding him all along. Satan, from the very start, was destined to lose, even though he didn't know that. And he's destined to lose when he goes up against us too. Why? Because he's not going up against us. He's going up against our Father, who can whip any Goliath in creation! Our Father has no intention of ever letting us go down in disgrace because a street bully like Satan wants to prove Him wrong! "Greater is He who is in you than he who is in the world!"

Things to Think About or Discuss:
1. The previous chapter could have been very scary. In what ways has this chapter offered you hope?
2. Do you think God has a hedge up about you? If so, what evidence have you found for thinking that?
3. How great do you see God's power? What passages help you most in picturing the greatness of God? What comfort do you find in His character and person?
4. Do you see yourself as enduring? What reasons can you give for your endurance? What involvement do you see God as having in your endurance?

5
When You Just Want to Cry (or Scream!)

As comforting as it is to know that God will see us through, the "seeing through" can be excruciating. After all, though Job may have had confidence that God would not let him sin or lose his life, he still had to contend with the loss of his fortune, his family, and his health. The only one he had left was his wife. And she told him to "curse God and die." Maybe Satan even left her alive because he knew she would be a hindrance to Job rather than a help!

It's the "working it through" that knocks most of us out. In the midst of many of the trials I've been through I've often prayed, "Lord, just let me wake up tomorrow with all of this over and me having learned whatever lesson I was supposed to learn. I'd appreciate that!"

But it never works that way. The more common experience

is the daily slog through a hail of pain rather than waking up as from a nightmare, stretching, and saying, "Well, I'm glad that one's over!"

What exactly do we see Job going through in the midst of this most incredible of all trials?

Many Cries
Anyone who thinks he can "grin and bear it" when he goes through trials is either deceiving himself or deceiving others. Inwardly, we all ask a simple question: "Why me?" It's inevitable. Psychologists tell us that no soldier in combat ever thinks he'll be the one to die. When things go wrong for most of us, our initial response is one of outrage: "What did I do to deserve this?" And, "Why don't You go after so and so, God? He's a real crumb." Or else we flop into the mire of self-pity and say, "No one cares about me; I wish I were dead."

Interestingly enough, these are some of the kinds of responses we find in Job. Job was human just like us. He had the same frailties, the same depraved nature, the same outrage that he was selected for such a trial. In some ways Job is a reflection of all of us. He crystallizes the human experience of suffering in so many ways I couldn't help but say, "That's me," as I read the book.

Yet because Job is couched in strange language and idiom, we often miss it. That's why I'd like to go through some of Job's cries in the night to help us visualize exactly how he felt in the midst of it.

Job's Initial Response
The first response Job gives to anything is one of remarkable faith and confidence. Job's sitting on his porch reflecting on all the good things of life when suddenly a servant bounds up and says, "We were out plowing your fields when the Sabeans attacked, killed everyone except me and stole every ox and donkey you have!"

Job's just reeling from this disaster when another hapless messenger staggers forward, "We were sitting there minding our own business when suddenly—whacko!—this incredible bolt comes out of heaven and burns up all the sheep and servants. I'm the only one who wasn't turned into char!"

Job's eyes are bulging out now and he's slumped in his chair, his heart pittering away. But he spies another loyal servant hurrying up the road and prepares for the worst. And it is bad. "The Chaldcans came upon us in three groups, killed all the herdsmen, and took every camel you've got. I'm the only who got away."

Job sighs with depression and wonders, "What could be worse?"

He hasn't spotted the next fellow, breathlessly standing before him. "Master?" "Master!" "MASTER!"

Job looks up. "What else happened?"

"It was your sons and daughters, master. They were having a party and suddenly this tornado came up real fast and struck the house. The whole place caved in, and they're all dead. I couldn't do a thing."

Job slumps into his chair and wipes his forehead.

But after a few moments' reflection and waiting for someone else to appear, he finally rises, tears his robe, shaves his head, and falls to the ground. The four servants standing there are fearful he's had a heart attack. But then they hear him praising God and worshiping. His prayer concludes with these words, "Naked came I from my mother's womb, and naked I shall return there. The Lord gave and the Lord has taken away. Blessed be the name of the Lord."

Is this man for real?

Yet the text says, "In all this Job did not sin, nor did he blame God." That means in God's eyes Job did nothing wrong—in thought, word, or deed. And he didn't even think, "God, why did You do this to me?" All he did was worship Him and accept his situation.

Frankly, I wonder at this point if Job is being honest. But clearly, this is God's judgment, not ours. This is the inspired Word of God. If it says Job didn't sin, Job didn't sin. That's the kind of faith and character he had.

The Second Response

Obviously, Satan's ploy failed. But he's always got another trick between his horns and this time he gets permission from God to strike Job personally. Only he can't kill him.

Satan smites Job with "sore boils" that cover his entire body. These were the same kinds of boils that God sent as a plague on the people of Egypt during Israel's captivity there (Exodus 9:9–11). Hezekiah suffered from such a boil (2 Kings 20:1–7). This single boil was so severe he was marked out for death by God.

God also warned Israel that if they rejected His covenant, one of His judgments would be to strike them "on the knees and legs with sore boils, from which you cannot be healed, from the sole of your foot to the crown of your head" (Deuteronomy 28:35).

Clearly, whatever Job's affliction (possibly a form of leprosy, elephantiasis, or leukemia of the skin)—it was devastating. As we talked about in chapter four, Job was in such terrific pain that his friends, when they arrived, could say nothing for seven days. He was in such bad shape that he withdrew from society and became an outcast. He spent his days down by the ashheap, sitting among the ruins, and scraping at his skin with a broken piece of pottery (2:8). What a miserable existence!

In the midst of it, his wife suggested, "Do you hold fast your integrity? Curse God and die." In other words, "Are you going to persist in this stupid belief that God is good, fair, kind, and just? Forget it. Curse Him to His face. At least get a little revenge out of this pain."

But Job entertained no such thoughts. He told his wife not to be foolish. "Shall we indeed accept good from God and not accept adversity?" Even in the midst of his agony, Job maintains his faith. He recognizes God's sovereignty and right to do as He pleases. The author adds, "In all this Job did not sin with his lips."

That's a formidable judgment. When you're suffering, it's so easy to let words of complaint, anger, revenge, and malice slip out. Which of us, even when traffic conditions don't go our way, has not responded with ingratitude, anger, and even cursing?

Yet Job didn't sling a single insult, complaint, or accusation onto the scene.

This condition persisted for some time, long enough for word to get out to his friends about what had happened. When the three "comforters"—Eliphaz, Bildad, and Zophar—saw him, Job was so unrecognizable that all they could do was cry, weep, tear their robes, and throw dust over their heads (little comfort that was). This was the way the men of the East expressed grief, mourning, and repentance.

When they reached Job's place, they sat down, hung their heads, and said nothing. For seven days. SEVEN DAYS! The scene is fantastic. Here's the most famous, wealthy, important, wise, and just man of the East reduced to a despicable, stinking outcast able to do little more than scrape himself off. Sitting about him are three men who care enough to be there. It's a deeply moving moment.

In the last year, my grandmother has been placed in a nursing home. I've watched her go from uppity and feisty to subdued and quiet to comatose. The skin has tightened on her face. I can feel the bones of her shoulders and arms when I touch her. She says little. When I come, I can do nothing but sit there with her holding her hand. But I can do it only for short periods at a time. These men sat there for seven days without saying a thing.

Cries From a Broken Soul

In the pages following, Job discusses his situation with his three friends, and then another named Elihu, and finally with God Himself. But it's in the argument with the three friends that the rending cries of the heart come from Job's lips. As time wears on and his condition remains unchanged, Job cannot help but question, argue, seethe. That's the thing that always gets us when we go through trials. If they were over and done, it wouldn't be so bad. But the sheer trudge of time and the lack of improvement brings out our worst.

There's no need to be ashamed of this. Even Jesus shrank from the idea of pain (Luke 22:42). Job hurt deeply. The words that fell from his lips during that time were the words of a desperate, broken man. It's through his words that we see our-selves.

"Why Was I Ever Born?"
Job's first cry was to curse the day of his birth.

It's almost funny. What good does it do to curse the day of your birth? To wish you'd never been born, or that you'd died as an infant?

Yet it's one of the first things we say when we go through great pain. "If I was destined for this, why didn't I die a long time ago?"

When I went through the depression I spoke of in chapter one, I often said to friends who tried to counsel me, "I wish I'd just wake up tomorrow and find myself an old man, having lived a successful life. I just don't want to face any more of this." At other times it was, "Oh, why didn't I die a long time ago—like when I was in high school and things were okay?" Of course, then I'd remember that I wasn't a Christian at the time, and shudder.

But I found myself going through strange and terrible wishes. One day I walked into my house, full of depression, and spotted my parent's dog lying on the floor sleeping. I thought, "You have it so easy. Just eat, sleep, run around, eat, sleep. Why couldn't I be you?" I actually spent days and hours wishing I was my dog, or someone else, or that my trial was over, or that I'd wake up and be renewed.

It's little more than self-pity, but it's understandable.

In the midst of Job's pain, he asks, "Why do I keep living if I have to live like this?" (3:20).

Again, that was a deep wish within me during my own pain. It was impossible for me to find any value in living like I was. Indeed, who would? If I couldn't be happy, why go on living?

"When Will It End?"
This second cry comes from the depth of a terrified soul. We think that if we only knew that light was just around the corner, or that an end point would occur next week, we could face it.

I often found myself praying, "Lord, just tell me how much longer it will be. Then I can take it." God never told me. Job describes the agonies he was going through in 6:4: "The arrows of the Almighty are within me; their poison my spirit drinks; the terrors of God are arrayed against me." It was as if Job's body was self-destructing. Barbs of pain shot through his abdomen. He choked on everything he drank and vomited it up. When he slept, his dreams became nightmares, and he awoke screaming.

"When will it end? WHEN WILL IT END?" we cry.

During my depression, I often took long walks, praying desperately to the Lord, pleading with Him to kill me or make it end. I'd sit down on the grass in a local park and cry, then pour over verses in Scripture, looking for that single magic statement that would zip me out of my condition.

What was worse was that there were days when I felt better and thought I was coming out of it. I'd go for a week or two, almost feeling normal. But then one day it would strike again. A creeping darkness would come over my mind. I felt it trudging through my body and though I'd do everything I could to stop it—take extra medication, pray longer, memorize new verses, enlist others' prayers—it would march along like a legion of soldiers up a street. I was powerless to stop it.

Then I'd collapse again in tears, crying out to God, "Please make it end, Lord. I can't take it any longer. Please do something. Don't You care about me? How can You let this condition go on? I'm useless to You."

It would go on like that for hours, for days, with no change.

"What Have I Done to Deserve This?"

Surely this is the most common response to suffering. We look around us, spot the wicked living in prosperity, going to restaurants, laughing in the street, and enjoying life, and here we are—miserable.

Job says in 7:24, "Teach me, and I will be silent; and show me how I have erred."

"Look," says Job, "if I've done something wrong, tell me. I'll make it right. Let's just get on with it." You comb over your past, present, and future, looking for that one act of evil that whipped you into this problem. But God doesn't say a thing.

You even begin confessing things that are ridiculous. I often began telling the Lord I was sorry for not saying thank you for certain things—like stubbing my toe, hearing the alarm go off, being able to see and hear. I asked Him to forgive me when I wasn't joyous and grateful for a "C" on a test. I went back to people and apologized for the most innocuous things. "Please forgive me for not listening intently to you while we were walking to class on Friday." Some of my friends thought I'd lost my mind.

"Just Forgive Me and Get It Over With"

Job reasons again with God, saying, "Why then dost Thou not pardon my transgression and take away my iniquity?" (7:21).

A variation on this one is, "Just teach me whatever You're trying to teach me and get me out of this problem!" We tend to think that God wants to cram this incredible lesson into our skulls. That's why we're going through this mess. "So give me the lesson already!"

But God's lessons don't work that way. If all God wanted to do was teach us a lesson, all He'd need to do is dump down a load of lesson books and be done with it. But the truths of life are learned only in the sweatshops of pain, not in the libraries of luxury.

"No Matter What I Do, Nothing Changes"

Chapters nine and ten chronicle the many thoughts and acts Job had taken to end his trial. He knew he couldn't answer God if God challenged him (9:3). Even if he was right, all he could do was ask God to be merciful (9:15).

He tried another tactic: simply admit that he'd lost the contest. "If God wants to prove He's stronger than me," Job said, "I admit it: He is" (9:19). But even that didn't do anything.

Next he suggested that he ought to prove that he'd done nothing wrong. Then God would let up. But Job remarked, "If I show how I'm not guilty, my mouth will condemn me; and even if I'm guiltless, He'll still declare me guilty" (9:20–21). So what does that do?

Job tried to use positive thinking about his problem. He said, "I will forget my complaint, I will leave off my sad countenance and be cheerful." But it did no good. He was still in pain (9:27).

Job suggested that they go to court about it. But again, who was going to decide between Job and God? God was the one doing it to him. There was no one greater than Him (9:30–35).

Job pleaded with God to tell him his sin. But God was silent (10:1–7).

The sense of having tried everything to no avail was one of the most difficult parts of my own trial of depression. I memorized more Bible verses than I ever had at any time in my life. I kept a rigorous spiritual schedule with prayer, Bible study, witnessing, and church work. I exercised. I took long walks. I meditated. I went to the doctor and did exactly as he prescribed. I confessed every sin I could think of, and then some. I watched my diet, looking for that one food that might be causing this emotional reaction. I was tested for hypoglycemia, diabetes, neurological malfunction. I took long physicals with blood tests, urine tests, kidney tests, liver tests, and tests on the tests. I wrote to everyone I ever knew who was a Christian and sent them prayer lists.

Nothing. No change. The same old darkness and depression every day.

"Why Won't You Answer Me, God?"

Surely one of Job's hardest trials was the fact that God was so silent. For years he'd worshiped God, loved Him, made special sacrifices. He'd received real benefits from Him, too. He thought he and God were good friends.

But now it looked like God had deserted him. Job pleads with God in chapters twelve to fourteen to simply show him how he's sinned. "That's all I want to know. Just spell it out. I'll make it right." But God is silent.

For the Christian, God's silence is undoubtedly the most difficult aspect of any trial. We all enjoy a favored position in this world. God Himself dwells in our hearts. We walk with Him and talk with Him along the narrow way. He's real to us. He's our friend, our Lord, our master, our brother, our God.

Then suddenly He's gone. No matter what we do, we can't seem to find Him.

For me, this was agony. I felt abandoned.

I battled inner doubts about the resurrection of Christ, the inspiration of Scripture, the deity of Christ, the reality of my own salvation. It had all become totally unreal and useless.

I told Him, "I thought You were a present help in time of trouble. Well, this is the time of trouble. Where are You?" I accused Him of not caring, of being a hypocrite, of being disloyal and unfaithful, of lying to me in Scripture. The next day I'd repent of it all, then be back at it the next week..

I spent long hours arguing with my friends over texts. But I was really trying to get a vestige of hope from their confidence. Yet God seemed distant. I couldn't "feel" His presence anymore.

I'd tell Him I was through being a Christian. I'd threaten to go down to a local bar, get drunk, line up a prostitute, then call up the president of the seminary and invite him to my party. "That way I'll get kicked out of seminary. See what You can do with that one, Lord." I was angry, confused, discouraged, destroyed. Nothing made sense anymore. Nothing seemed worth living for.

"I Can't Take Any More of This!"

Surely one recurrent cry is this one. "Lord, I can't take this for another minute. Please release me." Job says this in the poetic language of Job 14:18–22.

We're convinced that the pain is so great, we cannot endure. One afternoon my inner darkness was so overpowering some friends decided to take me out to a volleyball game. It felt as though something dark, black, and inky had filled my heart. I huddled in the back seat groaning and crying, "I can't take it any more. Please help me, Lord. Please help." My friends were concerned and kept trying to tell me positive things. But it hurt so much.

When we reached the volleyball game, I tried to play. I kept telling myself, "Be a robot. Ignore the pain." I even forced myself to laugh at the jokes and the play. But inside I was screaming.

"Nobody Cares About Me!"

Again, another self-pitying cry. We find it in 19:13–22. Job speaks of how his family has deserted him. His "intimate friends have forgotten" him. The maids in his house "consider him a stranger." He calls out to his servants and has to plead with them to obey. He even says that his wife can't stand it and tells him he has bad breath—get away! (19:17).

How can people be so cruel? Because they don't understand. To them Job had become a burden.

When I was going through this period I attended a wedding and overheard someone say to a relative, "What's happened to Mark? He seems so down. All he does is complain." I felt that people avoided me after awhile. You begin to feel totally alone. Which leads to another kind of cry:

"Nobody Understands!"

Job cries out repeatedly to his three "comforters," "Pity me, pity me, O you my friends, for the hand of God has struck me. Why do you persecute me as God does . . . ?" (Job 19:21–22).

It's not just that Job wanted sympathy. But he felt totally rejected, totally alone. It was only when I found some people who had suffered from depression like I was that I sensed I was not alone. Some of those people took me in hand, worked with me, loved me, encouraged me. Some wrote me long letters.

Perhaps one of the greatest moments for me was when a close friend spoke with me about a period in his life when he'd gone through a depression. He told me it came on like someone just turned a switch in his chest. It was the same thing for me. My friend seemed to understand like no one else on earth. But I was 1,500 miles away. And he couldn't crawl inside my flesh and make it better. I still went through long periods of fear and loneliness.

59

"Where Can I Get Some Answers?"

Job asks in 28:12, "Where can wisdom be found? And where is the place of understanding?"

He was asking another question we all ask in the midst of a trial: What is the reason for this? Who can answer? Where can I get help?

Our mind floods with questions. But few people have answers.

I began meeting with a professor and another student for fellowship, friendship, and lunch. But it soon turned into a counseling session for me. I asked desperate questions. "Why is this happening to me?" "What is God trying to teach me?" "Where is it all going?" "Am I meant to die?" "If I commit suicide, will I go to hell?"

There weren't many answers. My friends just looked on me with sympathy and tried to tell me God would see me through. But it felt like He wasn't. For me, He seemed to have disappeared.

"Everything Used to Be So Perfect"

In chapter twenty-nine Job looks back and thinks how things used to be so perfect. When he went out to the city square, all the old men stood up, and the young men became silent. Princes came by to listen to his wisdom. He was able to help poor people. He stopped wicked people and took up the cause of the needy. He thought he'd live a long life, die in his little niche at home, and everyone would remember him as one tremendous guy.

But now it's all gone. Job is wiped out, people who used to listen to him now mock him. Everyone abhors him.

How often during that time of pain I looked back and wished that somehow time could be turned around. I thought of high school, college, snow skiing, water skiing, going out and watching the deer. I lamented how I'd never appreciated it all at the time. "But I'll never do that again," I assured the Lord. I longed for the "good old days."

But they were gone, and there I was, broken and useless. Nothing could take me and no one could put me together again except God, and He wouldn't!

It was all self-pity. But what else do you do? I'd tried everything. But God had locked me in a corner in a straitjacket with a gag in my mouth, blinders on my eyes, and plugs in my ears. I was totally at His mercy.

"What Good Is It to Serve God?"

This is the final question Job asked. It's what we all come to.

In chapter thirty Job comes to the conclusion that there's no use in serving God. Doing good only resulted in getting back evil. So what's the use?

I remember sitting on my bed one afternoon, my heart teeming with darkness, anxiety, and depression. I was angry and gritting my teeth. I began telling the Lord off like I never had before. This was it—the end. I was never going to serve Him again. I was going to write a book proving Christianity was bunk. I would become His enemy. I'd have to make my way without Him.

After all those hot words poured out of me, I lay down on my bed and wept. I said to the Lord, "But I don't want to, Lord. I want You. I want to be out of this. I want to serve You again with all my heart."

Something within me knew that it was Jesus or nothing. Without Him life surely wasn't worth living. But what could I do? With Him things seemed to have gone sour.

For the Christian, though he may feel angry with God, and may tell Him there's no point in serving Him, he really can't escape it. Deep down he knows that the Lord is all there is.

The End of Job's Cries

Job is finally wrung out in chapter thirty-two. He's out-argued his three friends and now he's left with nothing but the same pain he's endured for weeks, possibly months now.

In chapter thirty-one he brings an all-encompassing curse upon himself. "If I've walked in falsehood," he says, "then let me serve others." "If I've lusted after other women, then let my own wife be another's slave." "If I've failed to meet the needs of the poor, the widow, or the orphan, then let my shoulder fall from its socket, and let my arm be cut off at the elbow." "If I've put my trust in money, then I deserve God's worst."

Job can think of nothing he's done to deserve the kind of calamity that has happened to him.

And ultimately that's the question that befuddles us all when we go through a trial. We each have this secret conviction, regardless of whether we've heard or been taught to the contrary, that when you do good, good things happen to you, and when you do bad, bad things happen to you. If we can't find anything bad in our recent or distant past, what is the explanation for all the horrible things that happen to us? If the trial is devastating, we're convinced that we must have done something truly awful. But we can't think of anything.

Thus, Job concludes that all he can do is prove to God he's done nothing.

It's understandable that Job would have these feelings, isn't it? We all have them. It's not sinful to ask such questions. Nor is it sinful to become angry and upset with the Lord about our turmoil.

I see that Job made only one mistake in all the cries he made during his season of pain. It was this: he continued to believe that he'd done nothing wrong; therefore this shouldn't be happening to him. His trial was way out of proportion to any sin he might have committed.

It was a simple mistake of theology. Job simply didn't understand the world from the divine perspective.

Yet, in the midst of it all, Job did one thing that ignites within us the greatest admiration and hope: he refused to deny the faith.

In 6:1 he said, "But it is still my consolation, and I rejoice in unsparing pain, that I have not denied the words of the Holy One."

In 19:25 he reminds his friends, "As for me, I know that my Redeemer lives, and at the last He will take His stand on the earth."

In 23:6 he says again that he's confident God will listen to him if He will only give him a chance to state his case.

In 23:10–11 he says, "But He knows the way I take; when He has tried me, I shall come forth as gold. My foot has held fast to His path. I have kept His way and not turned aside."

It's remarkable, considering what Job was going through. But like all who have tasted of God's heavenly gift, we know that ultimately there's no other place to go. Like Peter said when Jesus asked the disciples if they also would desert Him (when a whole group already had), "Lord, to whom shall we go? You have words of eternal life" (John 6:68).

That was what finally held me in my own struggles. Where else was I going to go? If Jesus wasn't for real, then I was lost. I had to stick with Him—even if it was agony.

Things to Think About or Discuss:
1. When you have suffered, what were your primary "cries in the night?" Where did you find comfort?
2. How do Job's first and second responses to his disasters strike you? Do you think this is too idealistic to be true? Have you ever responded in this way to a trial? Explain.
3. What were the main things that wore Job down? What were the worst parts of the trials you've been through—time, not knowing when it would end, etc.?
4. How have you felt when you went through doubts and asked angry questions of God? Have you ever gotten really angry at God and poured out your feelings to Him? Do you think this is legitimate? Explain.

6
Job and His Friends— A Dramatic Sketch

*T*he Book of Job is above all a poetic dramatization of a theological discussion. Its poetry has been called one of the highest dramas of our history. Unfortunately the power of its words are often lost on us. We get mired in the high language and come away thinking, "I guess I need the preacher to explain all this to me."

What I want to do in this chapter is to take you through the drama using common, concise, and modern American speech. This way you can follow the argument without losing its thread and meaning. Before we proceed to the actual argument, though, let me introduce you to the two debate teams.

Team one consists of Job, the boil-scraping sufferer. That's not to make a joke. In the midst of what you are about to read, don't lose sight of the fact that Job himself is a sight. His skin has become black. He itches and scratches himself constantly. His body is puffy and gross with running boils. He's sitting on a heap of ashes. He's in continual pain, and only rises above it to answer the insults and insinuations of his so-called comforters.

Team two consists of Eliphaz, Bildad, and Zophar, three neighbors who knew Job as the greatest man of the East. They've come to comfort Job but end up arguing with him.

Eliphaz appears to be the philosopher of the group. He makes observations of life, and on the basis of his experience, he comes to conclusions. He forms principles on the basis of what he has seen. He's the most courteous and benign of Job's comforters, probably the oldest, and certainly the kindest. His comfort is akin to one who dabs alcohol onto a running wound. When you say, "That hurts," he says, "Don't worry, it's good for you." He's a moralist, drawing conclusions from what he believes is ethically correct.

Bildad is more severe, a lecturer at heart. He relies on tradition for his proofs. He goes back to history and pulls out of it what he likes to make his point. He's good at setting up straw men and knocking them about like the wicked queen did to the scarecrow in "The Wizard of Oz." He may be the middle one in age. His comfort is like a nurse who puts sulfuric acid into your wounds, and as you watch your flesh burn, says, "This'll kill every last germ."

Zophar is by far the worst of the three, a virtual bigot. He doesn't reason like the other two. He merely offers high pronouncements. He's a dogmatist. His line is, "That's the way it is and if you don't like it, lump it." If Eliphaz pours alcohol on Job's wounds, and Bildad gives him sulfuric acid, Zophar is the one who takes a gun and shoots him, saying, "That's the best way to deal with this type of problem."

It's these two teams that battle out the most basic of all theological questions: *Why do people suffer?* Let's take a look at how they do.

Job is the first one to speak, after a silence of seven days.

JOB

I can't believe how bad this is. I wish I'd never been born. I wish I'd died the moment I came out of the womb. Then at least I would have gone to sleep and wouldn't have had to face this.

I don't understand it. Why does God let suffering people continue to live and suffer more? Why doesn't He simply let me die and get it over with?

ELIPHAZ

I can see how painful it must be for you, Job. But can I say something? You yourself have pointed out the right way to others when they got off the track. So I hope you won't be impatient with me if I offer you some words of wisdom.

The main question I want to ask you is this: When did anyone suffer who was truly innocent? Have you ever seen righteous people destroyed? What I've seen is that people who *sin* go through trouble like this, not good people.

Once I had a vision. I was so afraid my beard bristled. A spirit came to me in the vision and said, "Can anyone be right with God on his own? No one."

So I'm telling you, Job, don't be angry about all this. Everyone has trouble in this life. All you need to do is seek God. He'll receive you, forgive you, and make everything right. He receives people who humble themselves. He doesn't receive the proud.

Take a look around. Anyone will tell you. They were happy when God disciplined them, because afterwards they were blessed. And better people for it, too!

JOB

Hey, give me a break. If I'm being a little impatient here, I think it's understandable. Look at what's happened to me. God has hurt me. My body is on fire. All I ask is that God let me die.

But if I have to live on, I am glad of one thing: I haven't denied God or rejected my faith. But how long am I going to wait? I can't stand it much longer. Anyway, you of all people should be kind to a person in despair so that he doesn't give up the faith. But you're being treacherous. This is incredible.

I only ask that God show me what I've done wrong. That's all. Is that so much?

(Job opens wide his arms in an appealing fashion.)

Please, there must be some other reason this is happening. You're assuming I'm guilty of some sin, and I tell you, I can't find anything worthy of this pain. Have a little compassion. I'm just a man, not a brick. I could die at any moment. And I assure you, I'm not going to shut up about this. This kind of treatment is outrageous.

(Job begins to weep.)

O God, please show me what I've done to deserve this. Why are You making me a target for all Your anger? Why won't You simply forgive me?

BILDAD
(His face is red with anger.)

How long will you persist in blowing off hot air? Is God ever unjust? If your sons sinned, then they paid for it when the wind blew the house down on them. If you're innocent, then God will deliver you.

Just take a look at all the people in past history. They found out the same thing. People who sin perish. People who commit wickedness get judged. God would never reject a righteous person, nor will He support evildoers.

So I say, seek Him and everything will be made right.

(Bildad bangs his fists together to make his point.)

JOB
(Job shrugs as he begins and waves his hand in a conciliatory gesture.)

Okay, in principle I agree with you. God never supports evildoers. But how can anyone be right with God? If you want to argue with God, you can never win. You'd never answer Him in a thousand times. Even if I was right, I couldn't answer Him. I'd have to plead for mercy that He not punish my impudence. Anyway, if I called to Him and He did answer, I wouldn't believe it. He'd just give me more of the same. That's why I say He's being unjust. Even if I say I'm innocent, He'll say I'm guilty. So what's the use?

Sometimes I even try to see the good side of this and I tell myself, "Just forget all this pain, Job. Be happy anyway." But it just goes on and on. No matter what I do, it still hurts. It's a losing battle. If He'd just take away all my pains, then we could talk like two responsible people.

(Job looks down at his hands and chokes.)

Look, I hate myself. I hate life. All I ask is that God show me why He's angry with me. I've searched myself, examined myself, and I can't find any sin. Yet, nothing changes. I'm still in this pain.

(He lifts his eyes to heaven and pleads.)

O God, You made me. Are You planning to destroy me? Why didn't You let me die long ago if this is what I have to endure?

ZOPHAR
(He's been standing and pacing as he listens to Job. Now he stops and looks directly into Job's face while standing.)

I can't believe you're talking like this. Somebody has to answer what you're saying and I think I'm the one to do it. Can we remain here and listen to you, a sinner, boast as if you're righteous? No way. You say that you're innocent. Frankly, I wish God would come right down here and tell you what you are! God knows everything. He doesn't have to do an investigation to find out what you've done. I'm telling you, if you'd repent and turn away from your wickedness, everything would be worked out. This argument is making me sick.

(He sits and folds his arms, looking away in disgust.)

JOB
(Job stares at Zophar, tries to rise, but the pain is too great. He winces, then fixes Zophar with a hard eye.)

Well, now I've heard it all! Certainly wisdom will die when you die!

Look, you. I'm no idiot and I've observed some of these things too. But you act like I'm some sort of joke. It's easy enough for you to say. You aren't covered with boils; your whole life isn't ruined.

I know God's power and that He rules all creation. God has perfect right to do with anyone as He pleases. He even does things that seem strange to us. Sometimes He turns kings into paupers and makes fools of judges. He raises up a nation, then destroys it. I've seen it all.

But I'd like to talk to God. You three aren't going to explain it. Instead, you accuse me. I'd rather that you simply shut up than talk like this.

(Job pauses, then talks in hard, biting words.)

Are you going to sit there and tell me you speak for God? You'd better be careful. He may judge you. If you're going to be biased in your arguments against me, He'll have to correct you. And that won't be pleasant. Frankly, all your grand arguments are muck as far as I'm concerned.

(Job turns away and bites his lip.)
(He turns back and looks at Zophar again.)

Anyway, if I want to argue with God, what's that to you? Even if He destroys me, I'll still hope in Him. I'll go to Him and ask for an explanation. I'll never get one out of you.

(Job sits back, tired, and pained. Tears come to his eyes again and he bows in prayer.)

Please, God, answer me. How many sins have I committed? Why are You silent? Don't You care about me any more? Life is so short. What hope do we have if You're against us?

(He looks up with tears streaming down his face.)

O Lord, I just wish You'd let me die.

ELIPHAZ

(Eliphaz snorts and shakes his head.)

Job, you're an old windbag. You're being totally irreverent. Your sin is so great that everything you say only adds more to it.

I can't believe you refuse to listen to the wisdom of the ages. Let me say it again: Wicked people have pain all their days. They're hungry. They have no security. God is against them. They never become rich and their fields don't produce grain. It's plain as day, Job. Why won't you accept it?

(He fixes Job with a pleading but angry face.)

JOB

(Job stares at Eliphaz with renewed anger.)

You people are the worst comforters in history! Anyone can run a man down. But it takes some compassion to lessen his pain.

(He snorts and tries to fold his arms, but he notices his boils and winces.)

Anyway, when I do speak my pain doesn't decrease. When I stop, nothing changes. So what's the use?

And now it's even worse. God's handed me over to a bunch of bullies. All I do is weep. I'm covered with these sores, my bones ache constantly, my kidneys feel like they're about to split. And on top of it all, I have these three friends who do nothing but mock me.

(He looks angrily toward heaven and shakes his fist.)

God, above all I ask You to show them that I'm not guilty. I have no one else to turn to.

(He bows, shaking his head with anger and frustration.)

BILDAD

(Bildad jumps up and waves his arms and shakes his head with anger.)

How long are you going to argue? Be sensible and then we can talk. Why do you regard us as animals? You're acting like a total jerk. Let me repeat it again.

(Bildad holds one finger up as though counting out each word.)

Wicked people come to a bad end. They lose their health. They get caught in their own traps. Their skin is devoured by disease. God pours out fire and brimstone on the places where they live. Their own offspring die before their time. Don't you get it? Do I have to spell it out for you?

(He shakes his head again in frustration.)

Everyone in the East recognizes this and they say, "That's exactly what happens to wicked people!" What are you—thick?

(He sits down and folds his arms, staring at Job and waiting.)

JOB

(Job looks at each one individually with disgust.)

You people are despicable. All you do is insult me. I'm telling you, God has wronged me. I cry out to Him, but He doesn't answer. He's taken everything—my honor, my home, my health. Nobody in my family pays attention to me. I even have to yell at my servants to get them to come near. My wife tells me I have bad breath and she'd rather not spend time with me. Why can't you three, above all else, be kind to me?

(Job looks into each face, imploringly. When he gets no response, he shakes his head.)

(He looks down at the ground and shaking his head with anger, writes on the ashes.)

O how I wish all my words could be written down.

(He pauses, then his eyes sparkle with sudden faith and indignation.)

Just the same, I know that my Redeemer lives and one day

He'll make this all right. He'll remember. He'll make it straight.

ZOPHAR
(Zophar's face and cheeks are red with anger. He breathes heavily.)

Now I'm angry. I've listened to you go on like this, insulting us, acting like you know everything. And now I have to say something. Everybody everywhere from the very beginning recognizes that evil people perish quickly. Even though they love their wickedness, they get paid. Right away. Even if they prosper for a little while, it's not for long. God judges them and that's the end of it!

(He bangs his fist into the ashes, and little bits fly into the air.)

JOB
(Job signs and nods in wonder.)

Okay, listen to me one more time. After I've said everything, then you can mock me if you want. If I'm being a bit impatient, I think it's understandable. Take a look at me. I'm destroyed. Every day I reel in horror at what I'm seeing.

Now as for your persistent statement that the wicked never prosper and so on, I tell you it's not true. Many wicked people not only prosper but become very powerful. They have big families. Their offspring go on for generations. Their houses are safe. They have excellent herds. They sing and make merry. And they even mock God to His face! What do you say to that?

(No one answers, but their faces are hard.)

How often are wicked people judged in this world? Rarely. You say, "God punishes their sons then." Ha! God ought to punish them, not their sons.

Regardless, it's plain. Your whole argument reeks. None of it makes sense. It's entirely false.

(Job sits back, recognizing he's won for the moment.)

ELIPHAZ
(Eliphaz is upset and sputters a moment.)

Well then, if this is true, then why is God punishing you? Is it because you're so reverent?

No, it's because you're so wicked. You've robbed the poor, stripped needy people naked, refused even to give water to travelers, and have withheld bread from the hungry. You've been mean to widows and orphans. That's why all this has happened to you.

(He pauses, as though thinking hard and fast.)

You think God is far removed from you because you hope He can't see your wickedness. That's your real motive in all this. I see it now.

So I say, you'd better repent. He's trying to tell you through me that you must turn from your wicked ways. If you do, you'll be restored, your riches will return, and you'll delight in God again.

JOB

(Job shrugs and turns away.)

How I wish that God were here, or that I could find Him and present my case to Him. He knows I'm innocent and He'll hear me. Obviously, it does no good telling you!

(He turns and looks at the three.)

(Then he begins to shudder and looks as though he might weep.)

No matter what I do nothing changes. It just keeps going on and on. When will I ever see an end?

(His face twitches with anxiety and hopelessness. But he sees they don't agree.)

Still, I've kept His laws. I've treasured His Word more than food.

(He looks at a boil and touches it, embittered. Then he looks at the three with tears in his eyes.)

Frankly, I wish He really did punish evildoers the way you say. But instead, God simply tolerates all sorts of evil in the world—people who murder, steal, kill, plunder. God just lets it all happen without doing a thing. I don't understand it.

BILDAD
(He speaks with an edge to his voice, a sense of disgust.)

What more can I say? God is absolutely majestic. No one is like Him. Nobody can be right with God. If even the moon isn't bright compared to Him, how much less is a human being who is like a maggot!

JOB
(Job is still seething.)

Well, what a help you are. How you've opened my eyes! How you've saved me with your depth of wisdom! Why I think I could live on the pearls you've given me for at least a quarter of a second!

(He pauses and thinks back over the last few hours. He doesn't want it to be like this.)

Yes, God is great. He's done countless mighty things. He has set the earth spinning in empty space. He puts the waters in clouds. He keeps the sea under His control. But even with all these wonders, He says nothing to me.

(Job's eyes flash with anger when they say nothing.)

As God lives, I'll not stop talking. I'm never going to agree with you three. I am innocent and I won't back down on that point.

Now I'll tell you what I know about God. God doesn't listen to godless people. He will judge the wicked, but not on the terms that you've outlined. God judges in His time, when He sees fit.

Furthermore, I'll tell you what wisdom is. It's hard to find, but this is it: Wisdom is fearing God and departing from evil. That's the sum of it.

(Job sits back and waits for an answer, but the three are silent. He realizes they have nothing more to say. He feels bad about the situation and begins reflecting on his past life.)

How I wish I could go back to what was, when the Lord and I walked together in harmony. When I walked out to the gate of the city, people looked on me with respect. Princes stopped talking. Everyone said I was blessed. I helped the poor. I gave money to widows. I brought doctors to blind and lame people. When needy people came to me, I conducted an investigation and argued their case in court. I was a chief among my people.

(He chokes a moment, but regains his composure.)

But now everyone mocks me. Even lowly, needy people that I befriended treat me like dirt.

I feel totally broken inside. I ask God for help, but He doesn't hear. He's treated me cruelly, and He persecutes me. Haven't I tried to do what's right? Haven't I wept for hurting people?

But now everything's gone wrong. My only friends are the jackals who stand off and howl, waiting for me to die. My skin is black. My bones burn with fever.

(He looks from face to face, hoping to see some sign of compassion.)

Just the same, I won't sin. I won't even look on pretty women, lest I lust.

(Job's fire is returning. he slowly rises to his feet in great pain and looks to heaven.)

If I have lied to people, let God cause my crops to be uprooted.

If I've been enticed by women, let my wife become a slave for another.

If I've been unjust to my slaves, let me be dragged into God's court.

If I've been stingy with widows and orphans, let my shoulder be dislocated and cut off my arm at the elbow.

If I've trusted in money, let God Himself judge me this very instant.

(He waits, expectant, hoping God will yet answer. But the heavens are silent. He sits down painfully. He fixes the three with his eyes and he says with deep conviction . . .)

No, I haven't sinnned, I am not sinning, and I won't sin.

That's how I feel. That is what I will do.

✳ ✳ ✳

This theological altercation is not a good example of comfort. If anything, Job's three "friends" proved themselves more as enemies and fiends than anything else. They started off with good intentions, but things didn't continue that way. They moved from the *suggestion* that Job had sinned, to *indignation* that he would claim innocence, to *accusation* that he had sinned, to *condemnation* of him as a rank evildoer. Eliphaz even made up specific sins Job had committed without any proof whatsoever.

I once read of a sea captain who advised a young man, "Don't tell your troubles to others. Most don't care a hang, and the rest are darn glad of it!"

I almost wonder if that wasn't the case with Job's friends. They reached a place where they wished God would judge Job even worse than what was already happening.

Why did this happen? Why did good friends come to such a strong disagreement when one of them sat there in constant pain and anguish of body and soul? Most importantly, why was their argument so wrong?

We'll look at these things in the next chapter.

Things to Think About or Discuss:

1. Job's argument with his friends might have seemed a little more real in the paraphrase offered in this chapter. What aspects of the argument struck you the most? Why?

2. Have you ever tried to comfort a suffering person? How did you approach him or her? Did it go well? Did you feel good about it? Why or why not?

3. Why do you think Job and his comforters became so hardened in their positions? Did it have to be this way with them? Why or why not?

4. What would you have said to Job? Explain.

7
Where Job's "Comforters" Went Wrong

"**J**ob's comforters" have gotten a bad reputation in our world. Anyone who is accused of being one of them suffers an unequivocal put-down. It's like saying, "You're worthless." Or, "What a miserable friend you are." Or, "Instead of helping matters, you've made them worse!"

The first time I realized I was in danger of becoming such a person was when my wife became pregnant with our first daughter. For several months, she suffered from a debilitating nausea that stayed with her all day. She couldn't keep food down, even after the morning. It was so bad that the doctor thought it could come to hospitalization and intravenous feeding.

Often, when I'd return from my day at the office, my first comment, after spying the load of dishes still sitting in the sink, was, "Instead of laying around all day, why don't you wash the dishes? That'll make you feel better."

Valerie replied, "But I can't bear the sight of food. The very smell of it makes me nauseous."

I angrily proceeded to wash them myself, then said, "It's all in your head."

There was a lot of disagreement in those days.

It really hit me when we sat down to dinner and my wife threw up right on her plate before she'd taken a bite. I was so callous I just went on eating. I coldly thought, "She's just trying to make it look worse than it is."

My wife stared at me through bleary eyes. "You're the most unsympathetic person I ever knew. I hope you get pregnant like this and have morning sickness too."

It was almost funny! *Almost.*

But before you lambaste me about this and tell me I'm virtual pond scum, please understand that I've reformed. However, it does take awhile.

Nonetheless, I know well what it is to be accused of being one of Job's "comforters."

Good Intentions

These three men who first visited Job actually started off rather well. When they heard about their friend's disaster, they immediately covenanted to come by, sympathize with him, and comfort him.

The Hebrew words used here are interesting. "Sympathize" actually translates a word that means to move about with anxiety and be disturbed, to shake one's head with agitation.

In effect, what they planned to do was hear Job's story and agree with him. How do most of us sympathize with others when they're in pain? We shake our heads, saying, "That sounds horrible." And, "Yes, I really understand. That's the most terrible thing I ever heard." We become agitated in our concern and shake our heads with horror.

The word for "comfort" means to "be sorry." One of the Semitic roots even translates a word meaning to breathe pantingly. When a person comforts someone he may sigh and weep.

Their pain becomes his pain. He "feels sorry" for them and expresses compassion and grief over their agony.

That's what Eliphaz, Bildad, and Zophar planned to do.

When they finally saw Job as they walked toward him, they were astounded. No matter what they'd heard, this wasn't what they expected. They wept, tore their robes, and threw dust over their heads—Eastern expressions of mourning. These men weren't frauds. They were truly grieved.

One more indication of their own pain at the sight of Job is the fact that they were silent for seven days. This seems incredible, especially when we realize that the first thing most of us do when we see someone in pain is to say something ridiculous like, "I hope it's over soon," or, "I'm really and truly sorry, very sorry, so sorry. I really am," or, "I'm going to get the whole church to pray for you." Sometimes such expressions are euphemisms for, "Good heavens! You look gross. I mean, I can barely stand the sight of you. If I don't get away soon, I'll be sick."

Regardless of our plans, few of us could stick to silence for seven days. The compassion of these three men was true. They were the real thing. No one can fault them for not caring.

Trying to Find an Explanation

After seven days, though, Job finally spoke. And that started the whole argument I translated in the previous chapter.

After Job expressed very normal feelings about his pain, Eliphaz jumped in. He was very polite about it. But he dropped the basic bombshell that forms the foundation of their whole argument: the only reason people suffer is because they've sinned.

The argument went on through three rounds of speeches from Job and each of the friends. Insults were slung. Harsh words of sarcasm were fired out from each person. It was obviously an uncomfortable and unnecessary situation. Why did it come to this? Simply because Job and his three friends became hardened in their respective theological positions. They said, "You've sinned, Job. And you've sinned horribly. You've committed so many sins, they're piled up before God like a heap. Just repent, and the whole thing will be over." Job said he was innocent.

The argument clearly moved from bad to worse. Job's counselors started out well, but they became entrenched in their position and ended up accusing Job of heinous crimes rather than helping him.

Job's three friends found themselves supporting an unsupportable argument. They *didn't* know why all this was happening to Job, but they felt compelled to come up with some explanation. They had no proof of his sin. But they were convinced that their so-called divine principle was correct. They were the classic, "Don't-give-me-the-facts, I've-already-made-up-my-mind" type of people. Even though Job repeatedly showed them they were wrong, they only became firmer in their convictions. As a result, they moved from subtle suggestion to outright accusation. Not only was it possible Job had sinned, they were sure he'd sinned on a level that one could only describe as total wickedness. What then did the comforters do wrong?

Mistakes of Human Wisdom

We all make mistakes. We're human and so were Job's friends. *Their first mistake was to say that Job must have sinned.* It's true that God does judge evil in this world (2 Peter 2:9–22). People do "suffer wrong as the wages of doing wrong" (2 Peter 2:13). But God does not settle all His accounts on the day of the crime. Some people's sins follow them after death to judgment (1 Timothy 5:24). They are never judged in this world.

Second, the three counselors proved their assumption on incomplete evidence. They observed that wicked men usually suffer. Job was suffering. Therefore, he must be a wicked man.

But wicked men don't always suffer. Even Job brought this out. Sometimes they escape. Sometimes they even prosper in the midst of their evildoing.

It's so easy to become an accuser on the basis of faulty evidence. In any case of suffering, before anyone makes a judgment call on why it's happening, he first needs to get the facts. No intelligent doctor would put a patient on the operating table simply because he complained of stomach pains. It might be the anchovies from the pizza the night before!

Third, when Job argued with them, the three counselors became indignant. Job proved them wrong over, under, sideways, and down. But they only became hardened in their conviction that he'd sinned. They went from subtle suggestion to outright indictment.

Again, this is typical of human nature. When we don't get our way, we not only get even, we determine that we'll prove ourselves right if it's the last thing we do.

I remember hearing a Christian leader speak of a situation he was in while driving toward Chicago. As he cruised along, he passed his exit and his wife said, "You missed the exit, honey."

Well, that just made him mad. He said, "I'm driving this car. I know where I'm going. I know if I missed an exit."

She said, "You'd better turn around."

He responded, "There's no need for that."

Silence.

He continued on and the signs ceased to say Chicago. They began telling about Detroit and other cities not so close to Chicago.

She remarked, "Honey, all the signs for Chicago have stopped. You're going the wrong way."

He gritted his teeth and opted for one more exit.

When they reached the exit there was still no sign for Chicago.

His wife piped up again, "Honey, stop being ridiculous and turn around."

At that point, he decided to prove her wrong whatever it took. He began trying to think of a way to get to Chicago without turning around.

There was no way.

Suddenly, he realized he was sinning. He confessed his sin, gave up and turned around.

She said, "See how easy it was."

He smiled. "Now why didn't I do that twenty miles ago?"

"Because you're too proud."

That's rough, but true. When we get entrenched in a losing position, even though we know it's lost, we tend to continue in that position anyway. We're just too proud.

Fourth, in the heat of their argument, Job's friends forgot their original purpose. They ceased to be comforters and became accusers.

That's the problem with human wisdom. We become more concerned about proving our opinions than meeting the needs of others. This was the real failure on Job's counselors' part.

A friend of mine says his wife's chief complaint is that he's always concerned to win an argument. She says, "All I want you to do is listen. But you're determined to prove I'm wrong."

One day she shared with him a certain frustration with their children. His immediate response was to show her why she shouldn't be frustrated! "If you'd discipline them like I do, you wouldn't have the problem."

They argued awhile and finally she blurted, "Why are you always trying to win? Why can't I just air my feelings without you having to prove me wrong? My feelings are my feelings. Can't you simply listen without passing judgment?"

She was frustrated, but my friend told me, "You know, it's the hardest thing in the world for me just to listen. I always want to solve the problem. But sometimes what is needed is listening. Especially with wives."

I laughed. But it's true. When a person hurts, their hurt is valid, regardless of the reasons the hurt has happened. *Our job is not to show them why they hurt, but to offer them comfort the best we can—with love, kindness, understanding, and affection.*

Haddon Robinson used to tell his students, "When we go to God and ask Him why bad things are happening, He doesn't give us an explanation; He gives us Himself."

Why Is This Argument So Sinister?

Despite the problems the counselors had in dealing with a losing argument, there's another even more important question here. It's this: Why was their argument wrong? So wrong, in fact, that God told them to ask Job to pray on their behalf, that they might not be judged (Job 42:7–9)?

There are a number of reasons why this argument is straight from the pit. It's a lie of Satan that many people promote—a lie that does not have a single grain of truth in it.

It Becomes a Reason to Reject Hurting People

The first problem with this argument is that it divides and punishes people in the eyes of other people. It's virtually the Law of Karma, which says that people get paid in this life for sins committed in a previous life. What does that do? Go to India and find out. A caste system develops in which all the hurting people are set aside as gross sinners. Their pain becomes a reason to reject them rather than to care about them.

This was precisely the thing that happened with Job. Everyone began to reject him because they believed he must have committed some terrific sin.

It was the same argument we find in John 9 where the disciples ask Jesus why a blind man was born blind. They say, "Who sinned, this man or his parents, that he should be born blind?" Jesus answers that it had nothing to do with sin, but it was "in order that the works of God might be displayed in him" (John 9:1–3).

In their day the same argument was foisted by the devil on the world. Its effect was to divide the healthy from the unhealthy. The healthy felt superior because they were "good." The unhealthy were rejected and hated because they were so obviously "bad." No good can come from such reasoning. It's one more way Satan uses to pit brother against brother, saint against saint, and sinner against sinner.

It Turns God into an Arbitrary Gift-Dispenser

In such a scenario, God becomes little less than an arbitrary and biased giver of blessings. Where do we find that the good ends and the bad begins? How much good must one do before he's good enough to be blessed in this world? How much bad must he do before he loses that blessing? God is forced into the position of making such judgments for all the world to see.

Furthermore, what happens when bad happens to you and you disagree like Job did? You end up accusing God of being unfair. As a result, this philosophy destroys real faith in God. Lesser people than Job would have cursed God long ago to His face—which is precisely what Satan wants. How many people have rejected Christ and truth because they've secretly believed this lie of Satan?

At a train wreck, a father cried out and cursed God because his son was killed in the wreck. "Where was God when my son was killed?" he challenged. A wise conductor on the same train quietly replied, "I suppose He was in the same place He was when His own Son was placed on the cross."

Ultimately, this principle causes us all to become judges of God because His so-called judgments are so apparent.

It Forces People into a "Works" Mentality

Even worse than these thoughts is the fact that this principle teaches people to trust in their own works, rather than in the work of Christ. If you believe that doing good wins God's blessing, then you'll do good to get the blessing, not out of love for God. Doing good becomes little less than an exercise in selfishness. Real faith is destroyed.

On days when I felt terrifically depressed, even more than usual, I'd often begin scouring the previous day or week, looking for some hidden sin in my life. I became an endless nitpicker, concentrating on what I'd done rather than on what I was doing. My focus was ripped from loving Christ to wondering what I'd done wrong.

God has no desire that we live this way.

When I was in Mexico City, I visited a huge cathedral set on a wide square. All over the square people were walking on their knees. Many would take a step, say a prayer, or go over a bead of their rosary, then take another step. Obviously, they were convinced that doing this won God's attention and favor. But how can anyone think that God is so low He would require such demeaning things of people? It turns God into a wicked tyrant rather than the loving, compassionate person of Jesus.

It Doesn't Promote True Accountability

On the surface, this principle appears to offer a sense of accountability. "If you sin, you'll be paid back for it. So don't sin." But actually there's no real accountability. Too many people escape in this world. Like Paul said, some people's sins "are quite apparent, going before them to judgment; for others, their sins follow along after" (1 Timothy 5:24). We are truly accountable to God only when we realize that we will all one day stand before Him to review all that we've done. He will "repay everyone according to his deeds" (Romans 2:6).

If there was to be true accountability through such a principle, God would be forced to judge people immediately after each good or bad work. Our world would be turned into a tit for tat, "you-did-this, I-do-that" situation. "An eye for an eye and a tooth for a tooth" would be the standard of the day. When people saw that the principle wasn't being done to their satisfaction, they would be tempted to take matters into their own hands.

It Limits the Power and Person of God

Moreover, this principle limits God. It binds Him to a process that is impossible in any practical sense. He is no longer free to operate in human events as He sees fit in His infinite wisdom. Rather, He's compelled to make a judgment in each situation as it happens.

Instead, God has chosen to let all of human history run its course with minimal interference from Him. At the end He will bring about the great judgments which will bring in perfect justice for every creature. With this ahead, He's able to work within human events without distraction.

People Don't Believe It

But the ultimate problem with this theological assumption is that most people simply don't believe it. Evil people disdain it, being sure that they'll escape with the goods without reprisal. Good people note that it doesn't work out in real life at all. Why then do people promote it?

Because it's a simple way of explaining things. We like plain,

WHEN GOD SEEMS FAR AWAY

easy-to-understand principles. We want life to be wrapped up neatly, packaged and squared according to proper specifications. We don't want the interference of too many variables.

Furthermore, it's typical of many theologians to latch onto a principle because it *sounds* good regardless of whether it's true or not. People want everything tied together tightly and neatly so their leaders serve it up to them that way. That's the primary reason so many cults and false religions get started. A tidy explanation of things is offered. Simple minds accept it hook, line, and sinker for the sake of not having to think through the logic or truth of it themselves.

Recently I've been reading some books on the life and death of the people involved in People's Temple with Jim Jones. It's disturbing how many people were willing to submit to a hare-brained maniac because they thought certain things he was doing were good. A little decency in the midst of gross immorality held them. One family endured numerous indignities and slams because Jim Jones, they felt, was the first real leader to promote and provide social programs through his church.

The End of Such Arguments
Where did these theological mistakes get these three comforters?

When God had finally spoken, His first judgment was to tell Eliphaz, "My wrath is kindled against you and against your two friends, because you have not spoken of Me what is right as My servant Job has" (Job 42:7). God's wrath was kindled because all three of them claimed to be speaking for God. When one "speaks for" God, he'd better be sure he has his facts and principles right. Otherwise, he may win God's judgment himself.

Things to Think About or Discuss:
1. What have been the worst things Christians have said to you in the midst of a trial? Why did you consider them so horrid at the time? How do you feel about them now?
2. What do you find most sinister about Job's friends' arguments? What do you see as wrong with them?

3. Is there anything right about the way Job's friends argued?

4. Which issues raised in the chapter did you find most compelling about the wrongness of the friends' arguments? Do you agree or disagree strongly with any of them? Which ones? Why?

8
Human Explanations That Help

One of the poignant moments in my trial of depression came when I called my parents in the midst of deep personal turmoil and pain. I felt that all was lost, that I should drop out of seminary and commit myself to a mental institution. As my mother sat 1,500 miles away listening to me spill out my pain, I told her, "Mom, I can't take it anymore. Why is God doing this to me? I feel like a total failure."

"Mark," she said, "you're not a failure. You've graduated from a fine college and you're getting excellent grades in a great seminary. All sorts of people I know think the world of you."

"But it just hurts so much. Why doesn't God do something?"

"He is doing something. He's helping you through the doctors, through your friends at seminary, and certainly through Dad and me. God cares about you."

"But if He cares, why is this happening? Why can't I get out of it?"

"You will," she said. "You just need time."

"I feel like God has deserted me."

Mom was quiet a long time. Then she said, "Mark, have I or your father ever deserted you?"

The answer stuck in my throat.

"If we as mere parents would never desert you, do you think God would?"

At the time, I was so distraught the words didn't sink in. But they were an encouragement from a fellow human that brought comfort and hope to my soul.

I suspect that's why Elihu is featured in the Book of Job. God couldn't leave Job with these three miserable accusers. He had to provide someone with some insight and compassion. That's why He sent Elihu as the fourth player in the tragedy.

A Look at Elihu

Elihu was the youngest of Job's counselors. He'd sat quiet the whole time while the others argued with and accused Job. He did so out of deference and respect for his elders. But after chapter thirty-one even Job had run out of words. In the silence, Elihu decided he had to speak up.

He was angry at Job, because Job had repeatedly "justified himself before God" (Job 32:2). That is, not only had Job claimed perfect righteousness and virtual sinlessness, but he'd stated that God was being unjust and unfair. In Elihu's eyes, Job had gone too far.

He was also upset with the three friends because "they had found no answer, and yet had condemned Job" (Job 32:3).

He's acting as an unbiased observer and wants to bring some wisdom into the fray.

Again I'd like to put Elihu's speech into modern language.

Elihu Speaks

(After everyone has been silent for some time, Elihu clears his throat and begins.)

I'm much younger than you all, so I was shy about saying what I think. I felt older men would offer greater insight.

However, true wisdom comes only from God, and just because a person is old doesn't make him wise. So let me tell you what I think.

(He looks around. Everyone is looking at him, the three with some disgust and anger, Job with a sense of expectation.)

Now I've listened to you three older men. I've paid very close attention. And not one of you has shown Job to be wrong.

Don't tell me that God will have to refute Job. That's ridiculous. Personally, I'm not going to try. At least not with your arguments.

(He pauses and waits for someone to answer. No one does.)

Since no one will answer, I'll tell you my opinion. I won't be partial in any sense. And I won't try to flatter anyone. I'll speak truth, as I know it.

Now Job, I'd like to speak to you. I'm not saying I'm absolutely right. I'm a man just like you. I hope for that reason you won't be afraid of what I say.

You have said that you're pure, without transgression. You've stated that God has invented all sorts of sins against you. But let me tell you this, it's not right for you to accuse God like that. He's much greater than man and therefore does things we don't understand. Why are you complaining against Him simply because He doesn't give you a line-by-line explanation of His plan? God speaks in many ways to people—through dreams, through pain, through angels. He uses such means to bring men back to Himself and to give them the light of life.

(Job motions, as though to disclaim what he's said. But Elihu goes on.)

Please pay attention now Job, and let me say everything I need to say. Then you can refute me if you want.

Again you've said that God has taken away all your rights, even though you're righteous. You say that God has unfairly wounded you beyond repair. As a result, you conclude that it's no use serving God. Ultimately, doing good doesn't get anyone anything.

Now listen to me. First of all, God would never act wickedly or be unjust. It's His nature to be just and righteous. He can't sin. Could God ever rule the whole universe as well as He does and still be unfair? Never.

God sees everything people do. There's nowhere an evil person can hide from Him. He always acts with perfect justice. He has to rule with justice so that godless men don't overpower weak people. Otherwise, everything in creation would be fouled up.

At the same time, God does chastise all of us. He's not judging, but disciplining us when we are in error. That's why I have to say that I hope you continue in this trial, Job, until you learn not to be impudent in condemning God. Now you've added rebellion to anything else you might have done. You've actually accused God of wrongdoing. That's extremely dangerous and I exhort you to repent of that.

(Elihu is earnestly pleading with Job, and Job looks down at the ashes about him. He seems to realize that he has gone too far in his words.)

Now you say, Job, that there's no point in doing good because of what has happened to you. You may as well do evil too.

I say this: Neither doing good nor doing bad affects God.

You don't add anything to His majesty by doing good. Nor do you take anything away from His perfection by doing bad. Every person is responsible for what he does.

If you have prayed and God has not answered, it's because you've been proud, thinking He has an obligation to answer you because of your so-called goodness. That's plain pride. That's emptiness. God won't hear such prayers.

(Elihu pauses again. Job is shaking his head in agreement but he says nothing. The other three are astounded, but show nothing.)

I still have more to say in God's behalf. God is powerful, but He doesn't despise anyone, even the weak. He's never partial or biased. When He disciplines people, He does it only to help them and turn them from their way. If sinners do turn back to Him, He gives them goodness and prosperity. But if

94

they refuse to hear Him, they will soon perish.

Godless people, however, have it worse. Often they die in their youth.

You have to be careful here, Job. Recognize that God has a teaching purpose in your afflictions. He's seeking to make you a better person. Therefore don't resort to evil tactics in order to get out of it.

What we all ought to be doing is exalting God's work and name. Just take a look at all the things in nature that mark His greatness. Do any of us understand how the weather works, or thunder, or lightning? Take a look at this storm that seems to be coming up now. God's very voice is in the thunder. He's the one who controls the forces about us—wind, storm, ice. Sometimes He does things to correct us, sometimes to provide for the needs of the world, and sometimes simply out of plain love.

Do you know how He does these things, Job? Can you control clouds and array the sky the way you want?

For that reason, above all we should fear Him. He won't look on any of us who think we know everything.

(Elihu concludes and Job bows his head. There is a long silence. Then a sudden whirlwind comes up.)

The Main Points

What has Elihu said? I see several thoughts.

First, he's made it clear that *God is greater than man*. His ways are not our ways. For that reason, we shouldn't always expect Him to give us an explanation for everything He does.

We discussed this in chapter three, but it needs to be amplified. To demand an explanation from God for every little detail of life is preposterous. Even though God has good and holy reasons for all He does, we're not capable of absorbing what He says.

More importantly, the reason we often want an explanation is so we can agree or disagree with what He does. We want to pass judgment on His actions! We want a presidential veto for anything He might propose!

During my depression I often pressed God to tell me why I

was going through it. Was it biochemical? Was I supposed to learn something? Was it because of a basic flaw in my nature? Was God trying to build a certain character trait in me?

My response to all of the above was, "Well, if that's the case, then let's get the lesson done and get out of this thing!" To my mind, if I only knew what He was doing, I would then be able to be free of it.

I would often find myself passing judgment, though, on His actions. I'd tell Him all the reasons this shouldn't be happening to me. "If You're trying to teach me something, Lord, what is it? I can't find any lesson worth this pain."

Someone told me that maybe I was depressed because God was building character into my life. "Building character!" I retorted. "More like destroying whatever character I had!" I counldn't accept that idea.

Another friend suggested the depression stemmed from my summer high. "You were up on the mountain; the Lord had to get you back down to earth."

"Down to earth," I answered, "I'm buried a hundred feet under!"

Every time anyone offered me an explanation, I shot it down. What would happen if God gave me His explanation? Undoubtedly it would make sense. But I didn't want sense. I wanted to be out of my problem! Explanations don't do anything. And in Job's case, it could have made things worse because of the conversation with Satan.

The second thought Elihu has is that *God could be disciplining Job to help him grow in righteousness and faith.* God's purpose is educational.

We as readers know the immediate reason for Job's pain: because of Satan's challenge to God. But in the mind of God there could have been a multitude of reasons. Among them: to prove once and for all that people do not serve God for personal gain; to build into Job's life character and endurance; to give to the ages the book and story of Job to encourage us in our trials; and ultimately, to show off God's own compassion and mercy (James 5:10–11). Was all this part of a grand design to educate

Job? Could God show why Job's sufferings would become one of the great benefits and blessings in all of history—especially in the midst of the pain Job was in?

Though Elihu's argument is good, and God's plan always has instructive value, we should be careful of reducing everything to a lesson. If God wanted only to give us lessons, He'd have given us the Bible in sixty-six easy lessons instead of books of every type. Maybe He could even reduce it to fifty-two, one lesson for each week of the year. Instantly we see how preposterous the idea is.

I remember reading an article about a pastor whose daughter lost a leg to cancer. One of his parishioners commented to him, "I see now why your daughter had to lose her leg—because it has brought the church so close together!" His comment was, "What if the church started to fall apart? Would God take another leg?" Does God allow suffering on the scale we see it in our world just to teach us lessons?

Actually, it's the idea of a "lesson" that makes this thought hard. It's not really a lesson. It's a transformation that God is getting at. Instruction is educational. *Discipline is transformational.* Through teaching we become knowledgeable people. Through discipline we become godly people. There is a difference.

At one point in my depression, I sat down with my journal and recorded some of the transformations that had come into my life as a result of the depression. Among them:

—a greater sense of gratitude for little things
—a greater dependence on others and the body of Christ for help and encouragement
—a sense of God's majesty and power
—a recognition of God's sovereignty and the need to submit to Him
—a realization that the Lord Jesus was my only hope in this world
—a vivid picture of my own depravity
—an ability to empathize with suffering people

All those "lessons" I'd heard from the pulpit and read in Scripture. But through my own pain, those lessons were woven into my daily life patterns.

A missionary in Pakistan went through a difficult time when her six-month-old baby died. An old Punjabi woman came to her and said, "A tragedy like this is similar to being plunged into boiling water. If you are an egg, your affliction will make you hard-boiled and unresponsive. If you are a potato, you will emerge soft and pliable, resilient and adaptable."

The missionary remarked that it may have sounded funny to God, but often she found herself praying, "O Lord, make me a potato."

As simple as that is, that was what Elihu was communicating to Job.

The third word Elihu has for Job is that *God has a purpose in what He's doing.* We can submit to Him because we know that He's just, righteous, wise, and will never do wrong. His plan is perfect.

Though Elihu does not reveal God's purpose, he suggests that Job continue to look for it. More importantly, he exhorts Job to keep the faith even though he may never understand God's purpose.

That again is a good word. The Lord knows what He's doing, even if we don't.

When Corrie and Betsie ten Boom's story and suffering in the German concentration camp of Ravensbruck was vividly brought to life in the movie *The Hiding Place,* one scene that always struck me occurred as Betsie led a Bible class in the midst of the lice-ridden barracks. A woman calls out derisively to the group and mocks their worship of God. She says, "If your God is such a good God, why does He allow this kind of suffering?" She dramatically rips off the bandages from her hands and displays mangled fingers. She says, "I was once the first violinist of the Berlin Orchestra. Did your God will this?"

Everyone is stunned and silent. Then Corrie steps forward and says, "We can't answer that question. All we know is that our God came to this earth, and became one of us, and He suffered with us, and was crucified and died. And that He did it for love."

Love. Purpose. Meaning. God knows why. He can keep it all organized and right. If we will only trust Him.

The Best Man Can Offer
Elihu offered the best a person can say in the midst of human suffering. He did not know why God had allowed it. He knew nothing about Satan and his challenge. He only knew that God is always just, disciplines us to transform us, and has purpose in what He does. His final word is that for those reasons we should continue to trust Him and not accuse Him of wrongdoing.

It's not easy. But God never said it would be. He only said that He'd be with us in the midst of it.

Things to Think About or Discuss:
1. Describe Elihu in a modern context. How do you picture him? Can you think of anyone to whom you might compare him?
2. What strengths do you see in Elihu's speech? Why are they strengths? What about the weaknesses? Why are they weaknesses?
3. How much do you think Elihu cared about Job? What were his motives for speaking as he did?
4. Why is Elihu's speech only the best in human wisdom? What ultimately is wrong with it?

9
The Voice from the Whirlwind

When God breaks into Job's suffering and finally says something from the whirlwind, it's a startling revelation. On the surface, His speech appears callous, harsh, relentlessly indignant. But is it?

Again, let's look at what God says in the vernacular of our day.

God's Answer
GOD

(From the distance a storm is rising. The sky is dark. Thunder roars. Lightning flashes. The little group is ready to head for cover. But suddenly an actual voice thunders above the din. Everyone instantly knows this is God Himself.)

Who is this person who makes no sense? Who is this upstart

who makes long speeches without knowing what he's talking about?

Now Job, get ready, prepare yourself. I'm going to ask you some questions, and you teach Me. Tell Me, where were you when I laid out the earth? Tell Me if you know so much? Who measured it all out? Who laid the foundation and set its cornerstone when all the angels of God sang together at its beauty?

(Job's mouth falls open. He stares into the wind in the direction of the voice. The other three are quiet, but they appear overjoyed at God's apparent rebuke. Elihu alone is reverently quiet.)

All right, Job, now tell Me what you know about how the sea was bounded and assigned to its place. What keeps it there?

Have you ever gotten up in the morning and commanded the sun to rise? How far have you gone down into the ocean? Do you know what lurks down there on the bottom?

Can you control the weather? Do you know where I've stored up snow and hail for the Judgment Day? Do you have the ability to make rain? Where do ice and frost come from?

(Job's head is bowed now. He appears ashamed.)

Take a look at the stars. Can you make one of them fall? Is it by your power that they stay in place?

What do you know about lightning? Can you fire out a bolt at will?

(Job shakes his head quietly.)

Tell Me what you know about the hunting habits of lions. Do you provide prey for them so that they have enough to eat?

Do you tell the mountain goats when to mate and give birth? or the mountain deer?

What do you have to say about the wild donkey? Do you know why I made it free? What keeps him from going into the cities and raising havoc everywhere?

Or take the ostrich. Explain to Me why she does such an incomprehensible thing as lay an egg in the dirt and then abandon it. Does that make sense to you? Tell Me why it happens that way.

(Job is hunched now, weeping quietly. The other four all have bowed heads.)

Or what do you know about horses? Are you the one who made the horse so strong?

How about hawks and eagles? Do you know what causes them to fly so high or migrate from one place to another?

(There's a sudden silence. Then God's voice, having been loud until now, is soft and plaintive.)

Now tell Me, are you going to continue to find fault with Me, the Almighty? You've accused Me of being unfair and unwise. If you're wise, explain all these other things to Me.

JOB

(There is a long silence. Job is staring into the wind, his hair blown back. He is ashamed, exposed. His face is streaked.)

Behold, Lord, I'm nothing. What can I say about any of this? I have to put my hand over my mouth. I've already said too much.

GOD

(The response is sudden and fierce.)

Get ready again, Job, I'm not done. I have a few more things I'd like to ask you about. Can you really stop Me from doing what I choose to do? Can you condemn Me in order to make yourself innocent? Do you have power like Me and can you thunder with a voice like Mine?

If you can dress yourself with your greatest dignity and then go out and judge everyone who is proud, and tread down the wicked people where they stand, then I will personally admit to you that you have power similar to Mine!

Take a look now at the behemoth, which I made as well as you. He eats grass like the ox and has tremendous power. His tail is like a cedar, his bones are like tubes of bronze. He lies under the lotus plants to get shade. Even when the river floods, he does not fear. Could any person capture him when he's watching?

Or take Leviathan. Can anyone draw him out of the water

with a fishhook? Can you put a rope in his nose? Does he plead with you for help? Would he ever make a pact with you in which he becomes your servant for life? There is nobody so fierce that he would dare arouse Leviathan.

Just the same, who is Leviathan that he might challenge Me? Who first gave something to Me that I would have to repay him? Everything under the heavens belongs to Me!

(God's voice is thundering now.)

I'm not going to be quiet about this creature. Who can skin him? Who will open his jaws? When Leviathan arises, everyone is afraid. He won't be killed by sword or spear. Iron is like straw to him. Bronze is like rotten wood. No one on earth is like him. He alone has no fear. He looks about at everything and considers himself king.

Tell me your thoughts on these things, and then we'll know if you have the wisdom to be able to criticize Me.

(There is sudden silence.)

JOB

(Job nearly cowers, but he is no longer afraid. He bows deeply and reverently. He seems to have come to himself.)

Lord, I know now that You can do anything. Nothing You plan can be overturned. You have every right to deal with me as You have. Who am I to sit here thinking I know anything? I spoke too soon. I didn't understand. Listen to me, Lord. I will ask You and You instruct me. I had heard about You from others, but now I have seen You face to face. For that reason, I withdraw all my criticism; I repent here and now in this dust and ashes.

GOD

(There is a long silence. God then speaks to Eliphaz.)

You! Eliphaz! Stop a moment now and consider what you've said. You pretend to speak for Me. I'm so angry with you and your two friends that you'd better plead with Job to pray for you and make sacrifices that you might not be struck dead immediately!

(The three friends bow their heads, then beseech Job.)

God's words in this revelation strike us as harsh. Here is this man Job, suffering on a level that few, if any, men ever have. And God comes down asking him impossible questions?! "Can you control the weather?" "What do you know about the mating season of deer?" "Explain to me the thunder, lightning, making of snow, ice, and rain." On the surface, it almost appears that God is ridiculing Job. It would be similar to me saying to my three-year-old daughter, when she protests that she wants oatmeal instead of corn flakes for breakfast, "Okay, Nicole, explain to me the Pythagorean theorem, and then we'll see if you know enough to want corn flakes or not."

The Lord appears to be angry, harsh, unsympathetic. The statement, "God is love," looks like a lie next to this. But is it?

Whatever the Lord does, He always operates on the basis of love, compassion, righteousness, holiness, truth, and justice. If we fail to see the love in His words, it is a failure of comprehension on our part, not character on God's.

What Did Job Need?

To set God's words into perspective, we need to consider what Job needed at this point. For twenty-nine chapters Job and his friends argued about why he was suffering the way he was. Job became hardened into a position that said, "I have done nothing wrong; therefore, God is being unfair." It comes down as a slam on the wisdom, love, justice, and holiness of God.

After Elihu spoke, there was still silence. Job may have recognized that his attitude could be wrong, but he did not say so.

God speaks from the whirlwind only after everyone has had his say. Eliphaz, Bildad, and Zophar represent the kind of comfort the world gives suffering people up to that time. "You suffer because you sin." Job speaks for the self-righteous man who is convinced of the principle on one side—that good people get blessed by God—but when the reverse happens to him, he's outraged. Elihu takes up the middle ground. He suggests that we don't know all the reasons people suffer, but clearly the attitudes of both dissenting parties are wrong. The three comforters should repent for condemning Job without good reason. Job should repent for condemning God without seeing it from His perspective.

Sympathy Doesn't Do Much

What precisely did Job need at this point? Sympathy?

Every now and then I counsel with someone who pours out their story to me. Sometimes when I try to offer some perspective they'll become angry and say, "All I want is a little sympathy. And here you are telling me everything I ought to do about it."

Sympathy is nice. But it doesn't go far. To be sure, we're to weep with those who weep, especially when they suffer an irrevocable loss. We offer kind words of understanding, an "I love you," a kiss, or a hug. We say, "It must hurt so much." And "I really feel for you, brother." But that doesn't solve the problem. In Job's case, a hug would have been painful because of the boils, as well as a tender touch. Furthermore, his pain was so great that there was little any person could do except try to make him more comfortable.

Yet Job wasn't looking for comfort. He had servants. He could have stayed in the house in his nice bed. He was a rich man. But he chose to go out on the ash heap and scrape himself with a piece of pottery. Undoubtedly some of this was plain self-pity. Job wanted to make it look as bad as he felt. If he wanted comfort, he was doing everything possible to avoid it.

Furthermore, sympathy is something we offer when we are powerless to do anything else. A surgeon doesn't offer sympathy for cancer—he operates. A mechanic doesn't pat your hand when you have a flat tire—he fixes it.

God had the power to change Job's circumstances. From people sympathy helps because, after all, it's all we can offer. But God has the power and wisdom to change a situation. For that reason, sympathy from Him isn't enough.

A good illustration was Jesus at Lazarus's tomb. When He saw the tomb, He wept. That's sympathy. But then he raised

Lazarus from the dead. That's God.

Job neither needed sympathy, nor did he want it, except to be told that he was right.

Why It All Happened

A second idea relates to why it all happened. Did Job need to know the reason his calamity had struck? That seems to be the focus of all his argument with the three comforters. Job repeatedly asked God, "Why are You doing this to me? What have I done?" But did Job really want to know about Satan and his challenge?

Actually, what Job wanted was that God agree that all this should *not* have been done. Job was convinced there was *no* good reason for it to have happened. He wanted to know the Lord's reasons so that ultimately he could prove Him wrong!

We all do that at times. When I first saw a doctor because of the horrid depressed feelings I was having, I asked him why this was happening to me. He gave me three reasons. First, I had a poor self-image. Second, the stress of school didn't help. Third, I had learned to respond to stress by getting depressed.

I shot each of his "causes" to pieces. I only had a poor self-image as a *result* of being depressed. In fact, I'd risen a hundred points on the self-image scale since becoming a Christian. If anything, my self-image told me I was such a good Christian that this shouldn't be happening to me. I had memorized all sorts of verses, prayed regularly, knew the Bible inside and out, and was highly involved in church. Plainly, what was happening to me shouldn't have been happening.

Furthermore, I'd gone through two years of seminary and four years of college without incident. Why now?

And as for learning the behavior of depression, I'd never been depressed like this in my life. In fact, most of my friends told me that before this all happened I seemed to be one of the happiest people they'd ever met. I sang and made melody with my heart constantly. I was always full of gratitude. I submitted gladly to my leaders. So what was the deal? Why was this happening?

Obviously, my doctor didn't know. The reasons he gave me were simply wrong.

Wasn't that precisely Job's response? Every reason he was given for why what was happening was happening was rejected. Even though, admittedly, they were rather foul reasons, the fact remains—Job wasn't about to listen to anyone's reasons. He was convinced there was no legitimate reason that this could be happening. Therefore, God had to be unjust!

We always find ways to justify ourselves. Overweight people are overweight not because they're undisciplined in eating, but because their metabolism is different. People in financial difficulty are where they are not because they live beyond their means, but because their means isn't enabling them to live! Smokers get lung cancer not because of cigarettes, but because of fate, or because God has singled them out. After all, don't we all know smokers who don't have lung cancer?

When we go through hard times, most of us aren't interested in the reasons for our hard times, especially if our own conduct may be part of the cause. Rather, we prefer to prove that we shouldn't be going through such hard times to begin with!

Even if God had told Job about Satan's plot, what would Job's answer have been? Probably, "But why me?"

God says, "Because you're such a man of faith."

Job responds, "But what about so and so?"

"I couldn't trust him with such a test."

"What do You mean?"

"It's like this, Job. You're the one person in all of history in whom I have the confidence to prove Satan wrong."

"But how do You know?"

"Because I'm omniscient and I planned it that way."

"You mean You planned this all along?"

"Absolutely."

"Well, it's a pretty nasty plan, if You ask me."

"That's why I didn't ask you."

You see where it gets you. Job didn't want to know why this was happening. He just didn't want it to be happening!

How to Get Out of It

If there was one thing, though, that you'd think Job would want to know, it would be this: How do I get out of my problem? But I suspect Job wasn't even interested in that. In fact, how could Job get out of his problem? It wasn't the kind of problem you "get out of." His problem was loss—of possessions, of family, of health. They were taken away. He couldn't get them back (or so he thought). He just wanted to die.

Many problems are the type we "want to get out of." My depression was precisely that kind. All I wanted to do was terminate the depression. I didn't care what medicine I had to take, what verses to memorize, what books to read, what church to go to. Just point me to it and I'd do it. All I wanted was to be free. NOW!

But actually this is no answer at all. It won't be solved in a half hour like the typical situation comedy on TV. No problem happens in a vacuum. It's not a matter of "getting out of it." From God's view, that would destroy the whole purpose of the problem and of our existence. In fact, if God's purpose is only that we get out of all our problems, the answer would be to whisk us off this planet and lodge us in one of those heavenly mansions.

Job didn't even want to get out of his problem. He wanted God to admit that this should never have happened and therefore He should go back in time and do it all over! He shouldn't have to lose his possessions or his family or his health at all. Things should be returned to normal, pronto!

What Did Job Really Need?

If Job didn't need sympathy, to know the reasons for his problems, or to know how to get out of them, what did he need?

This is where God's speech comes in and why it's a loving, responsible, and compassionate answer to Job's situation. What Job needed was a fresh view of the majesty, power, wisdom, love, and greatness of God. Job needed to see once again that God was trustworthy.

In the midst of his struggles, Job became convinced God had been unjust. He felt God was no longer trustworthy. Therefore, God had to give Job reasons to see that indeed *He was trustworthy.* How? By showing Job He had total power and perfect wisdom for the circumstances of anyone's life.

God spoke to Job, saying, "Job, what do you know about how the earth was formed? How does the sea keep in place? What causes the sun to rise and set? Where does rain and snow come from?"

What could Job say? "I don't know."

"Okay, Job, what about this—how do stars stay in their places? Explain that one."

"Well, that's a difficult one there, Lord. I hadn't really thought about it."

"Tell Me this, Job, can you command the clouds to thunder and lightning? At your word can you produce a single bolt?"

Job looks up at the clouds and notices bolts flying all over. He bows his head. "Who am I that I might do that?"

Then God might have noted, "Job, if you can't do these things, what makes you think you can order all of life, even your life, so that it works harmoniously with everything else?"

"I never thought of it that way, Lord."

"Tell Me this, Job. Who keeps all the lions fed? How long does it take for a deer to give birth, from conception to delivery? And what causes the deer to grow from a fawn to a buck? What do you have to say about that?"

"Nothing, really, Lord. I just haven't learned much about these things."

"Then do you think you're capable of telling Me how to work with you, to make you grow, to teach you in the ways of godliness? Will you become My teacher?"

"No, Lord."

God went on and on asking incredible questions. Job needed to see what was involved in running Planet Earth. Once he recognized how great the job was *and* how well God did it, he was able to say, "I repent." He realized that if God was wise enough to keep the whole earth spinning properly, and all the beasts in their places, then God could also order his life and its details without a mistake. God could indeed be trusted.

Once Job saw how God kept everything running so perfectly, he could again rely on God to keep his own life running perfectly. God had to restore Job's sense of trust. He did it by exposing Job to His majesty, power, and wisdom.

During the days of my depression, one of the things I questioned most about God was whether my trial could have come from a Lord who was wise. I felt that God had failed and couldn't do anything about my situation. I was in the hands of One who was impotent to help. My trust in Him weakened daily.

But one afternoon in the throes of terrific psychic pain, I became convinced God would never ever be able to use me in the ministry again. I was a washout, a total failure. The summer before I had worked at a church in Hershey, Pennsylvania as an intern. One thing the youth group did for me there was to make up a little signature book. In it each of the young people I'd gotten to know had written a little yearbook-type statement that was meant to encourage and thank me.

In the midst of my depression, I picked up that book—for the first time—and began to read. Here were kids, counselors, and adults telling me how effectively I'd ministered to them. It was a staggering experience, as though God had planned this over six months ago, knowing how I'd feel that very day.

My last evening in Hershey, a young eighth grader came up to me and pressed a small note into my hand, then walked away crying. She had written, "Dear Mark. I'm one of those emotional types, so I wrote what I wanted to say on this card. I'm afraid I'd cry if I said it out loud.

"I wish you weren't leaving. But since you have to, good luck.

"A few weeks ago, we came to Wednesday Bible Study and my brother was making his usual remarks about how boring it would be. But you were teaching, and believe it or not, he came home full of talk about it. And now he comes all the time.

"I didn't know you were studying to be a minister until tonight. But I know you'll make it and be a great one. Love in Jesus, Meta."

It was the last entry in my book. As I sat there I wept. He'd planned that that very note would be in my hand that day.

I referred to that book many times during that period of my life. It became one of the many ways that the Lord said to me, "Mark, I'm in this with you. Just trust Me. I know where I'm taking you. Hold on, and we'll get there together."

Things to Think About or Discuss:
1. How does God's speech strike you? Would you like to be spoken to in this way? What notions does it shatter? Uphold?
2. In what ways do you see that God's speech is indeed a loving answer to Job's problem?
3. Why do you think God is trustworthy? What proofs have you seen of this (in the world in general and in your personal life)?
4. If you were God, how would you have answered Job?

10

Transformed through Suffering? Me?

*I*n *Christianity Today* (9-17-82) Ruth Graham writes a short anecdote about Malcolm Muggeridge who was speaking at a church in England. The local atheists had all arrived, prepared to revel in a unique chance to fire rounds at their one time comrade-in-infidelity who was now a committed Christian. Most of the questions revolved about the issue, "Why have you let us down?"

The rector finally said the time was up and only one last question would be answered. After answering it, Mr. Muggeridge noticed a lad in a wheelchair trying to speak. He paused and said, "There is someone who wants to ask me a question. I will wait and answer it."

The boy struggled, but could say nothing.

"Take your time," said Mr. Muggeridge. "I want to hear what you have to ask, and I'll not leave till I hear it."

When the boy's agony only mounted and led to further contortions, Muggeridge stepped down from the platform, walked over to the boy, put an arm around his shoulder, and said, "Just take it easy, son. It's all right. What is it you want to ask me? I want to hear, and I will just wait."

Suddenly the boy said, "You say there is a God who loves us."

Mr. Muggeridge nodded.

"Then—why me?"

Instantly the room was silent. After a long pause, Mr. Muggeridge said, "If you were fit, would you have come to hear me tonight?"

The boy shook his head.

Again, Mr. Muggeridge was silent. Finally, he said, "God has asked a hard thing of you. But remember, He asked something even harder of Jesus Christ. He died for you. Maybe this was His way of making sure you'd hear of His love and come to put your faith in Him."

"Could be," the boy said.

When we stand face to face with another's suffering, few of us are prepared to answer so well. But indeed, God may have allowed that lad to undergo just such a trial so that He might transform him. If it takes a tragedy to get a rebel to turn back to Christ in repentance, isn't that better than letting the person end up in hell? In fact, I have long believed that everything in my own life has been ordered for that purpose: to conform me to Christ's image. Paul said, "God causes all things to work together for good, to those who love God, to those who are called according to His purpose. For whom He foreknew, He also predestined to be conformed to the image of His Son, that He might be the firstborn among many brethren . . ." (Romans 8:28–29).

Though God had allowed Satan to strip from Job everything meaningful and dear to him, we know that God was causing all things to work together for good to Job who loved Him. While God allowed the test to prove to Satan Job's real heart, and while He sent the test to expose to Job the foundation of his faith, He was doing something else as well. It's the same thing God is doing when He lets us go through such suffering. He's building our faith and transforming us from weak, simplistic creatures full of false motives, wrong attitudes, and dreary hopes into resplendent creatures capable of exhibiting the true nature and perfection of God.

What happened inside Job through his trial is nothing short of remarkable. Job was transformed through his suffering.

Is Suffering a Legitimate Means of Transformation?
But here we must raise a question: is it legitimate for God to use pain and suffering to transform us?

I watched a movie on television about a small child who was kidnapped, mutilated, and finally beheaded by his attackers. For months his parents knew nothing. Then the boy's head was finally discovered by the police. Are we saying that God allowed that to "transform" those people, to "teach them an important lesson"?

Or what about the annihilation of six million Jews by Nazi Germany? Did that happen because God was seeking to change somebody?

Or consider something even more on our level. Are we saying that God allows accidents in which families are maimed or killed, crimes that leave aged people destitute, or earthly calamities like quakes, volcanic eruptions, tidal waves, and floods just to make us more like Jesus? When you consider that most people become less like Jesus as a result, you wonder if it works at all.

Yet Dr. Howard Hendricks once shared with a class about how in a meeting during a visit to India a leprous woman held up her broken and stubby hands. She said, "If it had not been for my illness, I would never have come to Christ. Thank God for my illness!" What courageous faith. Yet that's precisely the attitude with which we are to view our own pain and suffering.

Still, when we come to the issue of evil, most of us are repelled because it confronts us so personally. Yet God has chosen to allow suffering and evil to be a means of our transformation. Jesus was "perfected through sufferings" (Hebrews 2:10). Paul told the Philippians, "For to you it has been granted for Christ's sake not only to believe in Him, but also to suffer for His sake" (Philippians 1:29). Paul even said of himself, "For I consider that the sufferings of this present time are not worthy to be compared with the glory that is to be revealed to us" (Romans 8:18). He goes on to say that the creation was subjected to such suffering "in hope that the creation itself also will be set free from its slavery to corruption into the freedom of the glory of the children of God" (Romans 8:21).

What Suffering Does

Suffering is one of God's best tools for transforming arrogant, self-dependent sinners into God-honoring saints. This is because:

1. *Suffering makes us acutely aware of the power of evil in our world.* When we suffer, we see what evil has done. We come to hate it as God hates it.

2. *Suffering strips us of all our worldly securities.* Money, health, honor, prestige, and power can all go in a single auto accident. When we stand there in the wreckage, we suddenly see ourselves and our mortality. Only then may we have the humility to turn to God in true faith. When nothing else remains, He remains. Nothing drives a person to God faster than coming face to face with his own weaknesses.

3. *Suffering allows us to see Christ in His glory.* What is the glory of God? Creation? No. The Cross. It's when we see the cross and what Jesus bore that we can truly love Him. When we feel the impact of the same evil that He felt we can identify with Him.

4. *Suffering allows us to bear the fruit of the Spirit.* What is patience if not enduring evil people or circumstances? What is love if not giving when others only take? What is joy if not singing when your house crumbles? What is real peace if it doesn't exist in the midst of a jail cell or under the bite of the whip? Suffering is like fertilizer that bears the sweet fruit of godliness.

5. *Suffering shows us what we are.* It's easy to be patient and kind when you're the chef cooking the hamburgers at the local party. But what about when it rains on your grill and in your

Kool-aid? How do you respond then? It's simple to give 10 percent when we're raking it in. But what about when we're down to our last nickel? The knifing light exposes the dark.

What I mean is that suffering brings out our true character. If we're impatient people, having everything go perfectly won't expose our impatience; having things go wrong will. The only way God can rid us of sin is to expose it in the light. Once it's exposed, we can remove it.

How Was Job Transformed?

All this is good. But what about Job? How was he transformed as a result of his trial?

Job Saw God's Sovereignty

He says in Job 42:2, "I know that Thou canst do all things, and that no purpose of Thine can be thwarted." Job was saying, "I know You're in charge now, Lord. I know that whatever You choose to do cannot be overturned." Job acknowledged that God was the final authority. He answered to Him alone.

Furthermore, he was also saying, "God, I acknowledge that You have the *right* to do with Your own as You please. If You've decided to have me go through this trial, then I have no right to complain."

What a discovery! Recognizing God's sovereignty is critical to spiritual health. If we do not believe that God is in final control of every detail of life, then:

—We are in the hands of other forces more powerful than God: Satan, fate, destiny, or another god.
—We have no real security in God's Word. It's all a lie and a sham.
—We have no real security in what Scripture says God did for us in Christ, for it may be overturned at any minute.
—Doing right and obeying God are ridiculous. We ultimately answer to someone else.
—We have no reason to give thanks for anything that happens; since He is not in charge, He has no real control over it.

117

—There is no basis for real joy or peace in this world; nothing is nailed down.

—Evil has won, is winning, and will win.

—Nothing in life makes sense, for no one like the true God is in charge.

But Job discovered that God is sovereign. No one, nothing, no power stands above Him. If we trust Him, we stand with the one who rules the universe. No one can thwart, overcome, destroy, beat, eliminate, or triumph over HIM! "Greater is He who is in you than he who is in the world" (1 John 4:4). "All authority has been given to Me in heaven and on earth" (Matthew 28:18). "He is before all things, and in Him all things hold together" (Colossians 1:17). "In Him all the fullness of deity dwells in bodily form, and in Him you have been made complete, and He is the head over all rule and authority" (Colossians 2:9–10). We can give thanks for whatever comes because God is in charge and has chosen to allow that circumstance to happen. "For we are His workmanship, created in Christ Jesus for good works, which God prepared beforehand that we might walk in them" (Ephesians 2:10). Every detail and event of our life has been planned—not for the purpose of trampling us down, but for turning us into masterful pictures of Jesus Christ's character.

One summer as a teenager I visited Philmont Scout Ranch in New Mexico. I was terrified. Our leaders had played up the fact that there were plenty of bears and mountain lions in the vicinity. "Don't keep any food in your tent or a bear will come in and eat you!" You can be sure I didn't even have a candy wrapper inside my lean-to.

Then I met Buzzy. Buzzy was our guide for the first few days out. He wore soft moccasins on the trail, knew how to cook everything, could start a fire in the dead of winter even after an ice storm, and carried the biggest hunting knife I ever saw. I asked him why. He said, "For when I play with the bears." He planned to become a green beret and take on the world. Meanwhile, he was leading us.

Buzzy had a trick. He could make a shriek that sounded just like a mountain lion. "And bears is scared of pumas," he told us.

One night he had us gather up all the scraps and put them at the foot of his tent. Then he went inside. He told us, "Hide in the bushes and when that bear comes, I'll make my mountain lion cry, and you watch him run!" The bear never showed up. I guess he'd heard Buzzy was around. But believe me, when I walked up that trail I wasn't afraid of anything. I even walked along, saying, "Come on bears. Show your face. I'll take you on." Then I'd make sure Buzzy was still there trekking along behind me.

When I became a Christian I found out the Lord Jesus was a great deal better than any Buzzy. He wasn't afraid of the devil himself. For that reason, why should I be? Or you? When we realize that we're in the hands of the eternal God and no one else, that brings great comfort. He wounds us only to heal us.

Job Discovered True Humility

Even though he was the greatest man of the East, I wonder if Job didn't pat himself on the back now and then and tell himself how wonderful God must think he is. But after God spoke from the whirlwind, Job said, "I have declared that which I did not understand, things too wonderful for me, which I did not know" (Job 42:3). Job was saying, "I spoke too soon, Lord. I wasn't thinking. Forgive me."

When Job saw God, he also saw himself. He realized how little he knew, how weak he was, and how foolish he'd been. For the first time, he could bow before God and say, "Hallelujah, what a Savior!" and mean it with all his soul.

Humility is such a difficult quality. It's the one characteristic that when you most think you have it you most likely don't. And when you're unconscious of it entirely, it only then begins to flourish. It's the ability to lose yourself in life, in worship, in listening to others, in giving, in serving. It's abandoning your own desires and putting what is best and what exalts God most at the front. And it's doing it without a single lick of regret.

When Job saw God, he was set free to be himself. Why? Because he no longer had to prove anything. Knowing God was enough.

Have you ever felt that simply knowing and fellowshipping with Jesus Christ is about all anyone needs in this world? I like what Jesus said of Mary as she sat at His feet (Luke 10:38–42). Her sister Martha complained that Mary wasn't helping enough. But Jesus said, "Mary has chosen the good part, which shall not be taken away from her." What had Martha chosen? To be worried about all sorts of things—whether the dinner would go well, whether the beans were cooked enough, whether the gravy would get cold. But Mary simply sat at Jesus' feet and listened to His words. She wanted to be with *Him*.

Job discovered that God Himself was enough. Job didn't need anyone or anything else—even though God chose to give it to him. Job learned humility as he learned to love God. He became humble when he was able to say to God, "You can rule; I'll follow You anywhere. I trust You completely."

As a result, when we learn such humility, we can give thanks for everything, rejoice always, and pray without ceasing. Everything is from the hand of a loving father. Therefore, we can accept it with joy. Suddenly life no longer fights us. Rather we begin to slip along through it with ease and hope, knowing that God is blazing the trail before us.

Job Became Teachable

He says in Job 42:4, "Hear, now, and I will speak; I will ask you, and you instruct me." Job had argued, quarreled, won, lost, hemmed and hawed. But suddenly he was ready to learn. Why? Because he saw that God truly was wise. No longer would he tell God to "get it together." Instead he'd sit at His feet and drink deeply of whatever He had to give.

Teachability is one of those elusive traits that proceeds only from true humility. If you're not humble, you'll always have to prove yourself better than others. That means you can no longer learn from them, but you have to prove you know more than them. You become teachable when you stop proving your point and begin listening to His.

I find that teachable people are usually people who have been through pain. They know that they don't know all the answers. They've come to the edge of the precipice, looked down, and said, "There's no answer here." Then they looked up.

The life of Moses as you find it in the first chapters of Exodus is such an example. Moses began his liberation-of-Israel career with rank arrogance. He killed an Egyptian taskmaster, then tried to tell the people of Israel how to run their lives. Israel rejected him as an upstart. Moses ran for the desert.

For the next forty years, Moses was molded by God in humility and teachability. Moses discovered that he had little going for him, that he had wasted his life, and needed the help of someone far greater to lead him back to glory. Then God spoke from the burning bush. Now Moses was ready to listen. Even though he argued with God about going back to Israel, he still went. He still obeyed. He did whatever God said. Even when he had questions and fears, he ran to God as the final authority.

When I plummeted into depression, suddenly I became exceedingly teachable. My faith was shattered. I discovered I'd been running on "good vibes" for three years. I needed some rock to stand on. I read every book I could find on depression, faith, apologetics—you name it.

But what I kept coming back to was Scripture. What did the Bible say about this issue, that truth, that problem? I came to the conviction that the only reliable source of truth we have in this world is Scripture. Other people in the power of the Spirit can throw light on the Word. But it's God's Word that possesses power. Up to that time studying the Bible was fun, interesting, challenging, exhilarating. But when life caved in and I groped about the ruins, the Word became my pickaxe, lunchbox, and live-in doctor. All other diversions became inconsequential. Knowing His Word became a passion.

I believe real teachability only comes out of real pain. Until the Lord presses us to the wall, we'll continue to roll on down the pike without considering where we're headed. Like C.S. Lewis says, *Pain is God's megaphone. He uses it to get our attention.*

Job Saw God

Job says in 42:5, "I have heard of Thee by the hearing of the ear; but now my eye sees Thee."

How many of us live in the first half of that verse and never get to the second half? Like most of humanity, Job heard the principles and truths about God passed along from generation to generation. He heeded what he learned and tried to obey. He made sacrifices to God for sin. He treasured the few words he had. But through his trial, Job experienced God. He came face to face with the deity. God was no longer a person in a book, a name on a page. He wasn't this distant "force" or "thing." Now He was a comrade in arms, a king, a living potentate whose hand rested on Job's shoulder.

Have you made that transition? Sure, you have all these good feelings. You go to church. You give your testimony. When you were born again something happened inside. But have you seen His majesty, His glory, His perfection?

Despite everything Moses had seen of God through all the plagues of Egypt, the miracles in the wilderness and at the Red Sea, Moses was still hungry. In Exodus 33:18 he cries to God, "Show me Thy glory." What did God show him?

One might think it was an incredible light show, an earthquake or two, or maybe this monstrous person sitting on a throne. But it was nothing of the sort. Rather God passed before Moses and declared His attributes. "The Lord, the Lord God, compassionate and gracious, slow to anger, and abounding in lovingkindness, who keeps lovingkindness for thousands, who forgives iniquity, transgression and sin; yet He will by no means leave the guilty unpunished . . ." (Exodus 34:6–7). Look at it.

—*Compassionate.* The One who treats all His people with tenderness, like a mother with a new baby.
—*Gracious.* The One who gives and keeps on giving great

gifts to those who could never deserve anything but condemnation.

—*Slow to anger.* How long can you bear with people who slander your name, threaten you, and hate you? God has borne with such people for thousands of years!

—*Abounding in lovingkindness.* The One overflowing with the milk of kindness and love.

—*Who forgives.* What did it cost Him to be able to do that? The death of Jesus on a cross.

—*Who will judge.* The One to whom we all answer.

You could write a whole book on this passage alone. Have you seen what these words mean, how they relate to the way God rules the universe? Have you seen Jesus in that light? Or is He simply a person who gives you "good feelings"?

Prior to my depression, I spoke of Jesus as this great person who had done so much for me. Peace. Joy. Hope. An end to loneliness. Security.

When I became mired in the darkness, though, I began looking for the real power of the Light. For the first time I was forced to consider what it meant that God is love, God is majestic, He is Lord, He is sovereign. I was forced to reckon with whom I was dealing.

It's so easy to allow our relationship with God to cruise along with a virtual take-it-or-leave-it attitude. Sure, we don't say it that way. But how much time do we spend with Him? How many of us meditate on His Word daily? What's our prayer life like?

It was through depression that I saw that prayer was the mainstay, the Word the foundation, and walking with Him the only necessity. He became first in my life like never before.

I remember well the climax of my two and a half years of depression. It came one afternoon in my little room in a large house full of seminary students. I had come to the end of everything. I'd tried doctors, medication, memorizing the Word, prayer—every device I could muster to get me out of my condition. Nothing worked.

In the meantime, I had studied the Hebrew and Greek texts,

hashed through my convictions, and laid a foundation of truth that I'd never known before. I was more convinced than ever that Jesus lived, died for my sins, rose from the dead, reigned from heaven, had given us His Word, and was in absolute control of everything in history.

Despite it all I was still depressed. But I had come to a new conviction, something I never saw before. It came out in my prayer. I knelt by my bed. My whole body shaking and weeping, I told the Lord, "Father, I've tried everything I know. But You must want me to be like this. I don't know why. I have no more answers. But I want You to know that I trust You absolutely. I know that You love me and that this trial is from a heart of love. I know that You have a perfect plan and that this plan has not been disrupted by my depression. I know that You will see me through to the end."

I paused, took a deep breath, and then I uttered words that I thought I'd never say. "Lord, I don't deserve anything from You. But I want You to know that even if You don't take this trial away, even if I must remain depressed like this for the rest of my life, and even if my misery only becomes worse, I will continue to serve You and love You and obey You just the same. No matter what. I only ask that You give me grace to keep going on."

To that point I'd made similar confessions, but they were simply manipulative devices to get God to zing me out of my problem. I thought if I just said it, He'd relent. But this time I wasn't just saying it. I knew I meant it. I knew it was the end.

And the beginning.

Two months later I was completely back to normal.

I can't explain it. My doctor can't explain it. But I was transformed. God had done something marvelous. I had seen God as He was, not as I imagined Him to be.

That's the same thing He did with Job.

It's what He's also doing with you.

Things to Think About or Discuss:
1. Why do you think God uses suffering so much to transform His saints? Why is it such an effective tool?

2. How would you define humility? When Job became truly humble, what was he like? Why would you want to be like that? What do you think it would take to get you to that point?

3. What causes people to be teachable? Are you a teachable person? Why or why not?

4. How do you see God? How has your concept of Him changed over the years? How was it changed through a period of suffering?

11
Looking for the Good

The first promise many of us cling to when we go through hard times is Romans 8:28. We've memorized it. We can recite it. We remind one another of it. And we hold it sacred and dear, perhaps above many other verses of Scripture.

And no wonder. It speaks words of great assurance and hope to anyone on the precipice walls. "We know that God causes all things to work together for good to those who love God, to those who are called according to His purpose" (Romans 8:28).

A preacher could divide the verse tidily into several elements.

First, we "know." We're sure of something.

Second, "God causes all things to work together for good." He's in charge. Somehow He gets every event and detail, even the bad ones, to work harmoniously towards a goal—the "good," that which is beautiful, right, and perfect to the core. No element of the result is tainted. That doesn't mean all things *are* good. But everything works together to *produce something good.* Who then is this for?

Third, the promise is for "those who love God, for those who are called according to His purpose." There's man's side of it: only those who truly love God will see Him cause all things to work together for good. But some could *say* they love God when they don't. Thus, there's the divine side, for "those who are called." God Himself must have personally "called" you into a relationship for this verse to apply in your behalf. You must be born again.

It's a wonderful promise. Which of us who loves Jesus Christ and has been called by His Spirit would sneer in the face of this awesome power and privilege? Ultimately, it means that nothing in this life can do us in. Nothing can make life go sour, so long as we continue to walk with Him.

Yet, when we're going through the fire, this verse can seem to mock us. My first reply to all who would tell me this truth during my times of suffering was, "How can this be working for good?"

I couldn't see how. And frankly, they couldn't tell me.

It's like being in a boat in a storm. We're so busy fighting for our lives, bailing the boat, and praying for a break in the torrent that all we can see is the grim prospect of going down with the ship. It's only after the storm has calmed and we can look around that we begin to see what was really accomplished, what good came. Then we recognize how our fellowship was built with our fellow boatmen, how we prayed so fiercely and passionately for the first time in our lives, how we learned to cooperate and love one another. But this usually only comes *after* we've traversed the lake. Sometimes you have to get past a trial to see how God used it in your life.

Then what about Job? What good came from his trial? What if, instead of arguing with him, the four people who came to comfort him had said, "Look, Job, we admit it appears awful right now. But take courage, God will even use this for good in your life. We can't see how now. But that's His promise. Can you trust Him to do that?"

Maybe Job might have answered, "You know, you're right. God's always been trustworthy before. I'll hang in there and tough it out. I know one day He'll show all this as part of a perfect plan."

In fact, Job did say something similar in Job 23:1: "When he has tried me, I shall come forth as gold." Job recognized even in the midst of his agony that God was removing the dross and turning him to gold.

But let's look in more detail at some of the incredible results God brought about in his life.

Increased Fortune and Health

The most obvious change that came after Job's trial was an increase in his fortunes, health, and family. His family and friends responded by giving gifts, consoling him, and comforting him afterwards (42:11). All his possessions were doubled (42:12). His wife bore him seven more sons and three daughters (42:13). These daughters were the most beautiful in all the land (42:15). Job lived another one hundred and forty years and died, "an old man and full of days" (42:16–17). That expression means Job was a man absolutely fulfilled in life, chock full of good memories and cheer.

We're almost tempted to respond to this by saying, " God felt so guilty about it all that He lavished this on Job." But God wasn't acting out of guilt; rather out of love. He is "full of compassion and is merciful" says James (5:10–11) and the story of Job proves it. Job had proved himself faithful. The Lord wanted to reward him handsomely.

God is "gracious to whom He wants to be gracious" (Exodus 33:19). He loves to give His gifts "generously and without reproach" (James 1:5). In fact, part of the reason He's destined us for heaven is that He might "show the surpassing riches of His grace in kindness toward us in Christ Jesus" (Ephesians 2:7). He's like a billionaire who wants to use his wealth simply to make others happy. Only in this case, His fortune is infinite and His desire is boundless.

Another response we might give to this is that it doesn't happen to everyone. Many people's suffering seems to go on right up to the end of life.

That's true. But for all who love God, this life is not the end. It's hardly even the beginning. Like the great hymn says, "When we've been there ten thousand years bright shining as the sun, we've no less days to sing God's praise than when we've first begun."

Furthermore, for many there is restoration of fortune, health, and life. James says, "Blessed is a man who perseveres under trial, for once he has been approved he will receive the crown of life, which God has promised to those who love Him" (James 1:12). This "crown of life" is not a physical, material crown, but a spiritual one. Once we've proven ourselves enduring in faith in the midst of a trial, God rewards us with an ability to live a quality of life far beyond anything we'd ever achieved previously.

When I first became a Christian, I thought nothing could be better than what I was experiencing. But since then I've witnessed the Lord's work in refining and shaping me through trials. As I pass through each one I reach a higher plane of joy, peace, and fruitbearing. Life becomes even richer and more resplendent.

True Empathy

A second "good" that came out of Job's suffering was empathy—the ability to put yourself into another person's situation and see it through his eyes. As the Indians used to say, "Walk a mile in his moccasins and then you'll understand why he does what he does."

Real empathy is so hard. We're all so strongly focused on ourselves, our needs, our concerns.

I suspect that Job was not always an especially empathetic person. I wonder if he didn't make some of the same kinds of insensitive comments his comforters made when he went to

sufferers to comfort them. But having gone through his trial,
Job reaches a higher level of concern and love for his fellowman.
He doesn't hesitate to pray for his three friends that God might
not destroy them (Job 42:7–10). I suspect that Job became newly
tender and understanding in all relationships.

When you were in pain and you screamed out your complaints
and doubts at others, did someone ever say (or did you say it
yourself), "Just have faith, brother. Faith'll keep you going?"

When we look through the blur of our pain and tears, and ask
a well-meaning friend, "Why is this happening to me?" have you
ever gotten (or given) answers like this:

—"God is trying to teach you something. So try to find out
what it is."
—"You're probably worn out. Just get a good night's sleep
and you'll feel better."
—"You're not on a proper diet. Start eating right and you'll
be better in no time."
—"Have you been taking vitamins?"
—"Do you exercise every day?"
—"Have you been having your quiet time?"

Interestingly enough, Job's friends did the same thing to Job,
except they told him point-blank, "Obviously, you've sinned. So
confess your sin and God will make it all better."

Job responded, "For the despairing man there should be kindness from his friend" (6:14). In other words, "Gee, guys, don't
you have anything kind to say?"

As their assault intensified, he said, "I am a joke to my friends"
(12:4). "Sorry comforters are you all" (16:2). "How long will
you torment me, and crush me with words? These ten times
you have insulted me" (19:2–3). "What a help you are to the
weak . . . What counsel you have given to one without wisdom!"
(26:2–3).

Job was screaming for help, a kind word, a little sympathy,
and all his friends could do was reiterate over and over, "You

must have sinned . . . you must have sinned . . . you must have sinned."

But it's when we go through the fire ourselves that we learn to empathize with people who hurt. When we find out what it is like to ask answerless questions, to cry for relief, to lie helpless and hopeless on a bed of destruction then we are able to come to the aid of others.

Paul simplified comfort into a single sentence: "Weep with those who weep."

It's such a difficult truth to apply. We want to offer counsel, tell the sufferer how to get out of the pain, and contrive an explanation for why it's happening. Yet, most of the time all the hurting person wants is a listening ear, an open heart, a bit of sympathy.

I was hit with this again recently when I dragged home from work, convinced that I was a total washout as a Christian, husband, father, son, and everything else. I walked into our apartment, kissed my wife, tousled the baby's hair, and then crashed onto our couch, staring blankly into myself. My wife walked in, took one look, and said, "What's the matter?"

I said, "Oh, nothing."

She sat down. "Tell me."

I told her. "I'm doing such a lousy job at work. I don't know why they promoted me. I'm just a big zero."

She started to tell me that what I was saying wasn't true. Look at all the wonderful things I'd accomplished!

What was my response? I made some sarcastic comments.

In a few moments we were both angry, and I fired some more frustrated words at her, arguing with everything she said. Suddenly she stopped and looked at me through her tears, saying, "I'm sorry. I should have listened. Tell me about it." Quietly, she put her arm around me and I told her. Together we wept. Finally, she just hugged me and said, "I love you. I want to work with you through this."

It's amazing to me even now. I felt comforted. I felt as though she understood. She didn't try to give me three ways to stop feeling like a zero with proof texts. She didn't have any lofty words of wisdom. We just wept, listened, and exchanged words of love.

You have to go through pain before you can help others in pain. I suspect that after Job's experience, he was able to comfort others in a way he had never been able to before.

Life Is More than Being Satisfied

Job found out something else in the course of his miseries. In 29:18 he says, "I thought, 'I shall die in my nest and I shall multiply my days as the sand.' "

Before disaster struck, Job had it all worked out. He'd been living in fantasyland for many years. "I'll grow up, marry a pretty lady, have beautiful children, build my dream house with a brick fireplace and an eagle over the mantle, run a brisk business, become a grandfather, and die, a happy old man with my family gathered around my bed."

But God is not in the dream business; He's in the reality business. He wants us not only to understand what good is, but also what evil is—a monstrous thing that exists in our world. To woo us, as free creatures, to Himself and bring us to the place where we'll be utterly loyal to Him, He must teach us to hate evil. Once we see evil as He does, and utterly loathe it, then and only then are we ready to rule with Him in His kingdom.

Furthermore, life is much more than just being content or happy. It's more than self-satisfaction.

What had happened to Job was something that happens to most of us when we first start to walk with Jesus. We start to think we've arrived, that things could only get better and better, that it's "smooth sailing till we hit the harbor of heaven." But God has to shake that cockiness, pride, and self-satisfaction out of us. He wants to give us true humility, love, and joy so that we might "have life and have it abundantly" (John 10:10). The only way for Him to give us such a brand of life is to take us through the troughs, through the darkness of suffering.

Confronting the Great Questions

When Job was "down and out," he was forced to wrestle with the great questions. He asked lots of questions and confronted these issues:

—"Why does God let people linger on who are in pain, and take others who want to live?" (chapter 3)

—"Why does God let good people suffer?" (chapters 6–7)

—"Why doesn't God answer when we pray? And why does He tarry?" (chapter 9)

—"Why do the wicked prosper and good people fail?" (chapter 10)

—"Why does God hide Himself when we are in the direst pain?" (chapter 13)

—"What happens when a man dies? Is there hope for him after death (chapters 16–17)

—"If righteous people suffer harm at the hand of God, why serve God in the first place?" (chapter 21)

—"Why doesn't God always punish the wicked in this life?" (chapter 24)

—"Where can anyone get answers to the questions that are tearing our souls out?" (chapter 28)

Such questions occur to all of us when we suffer. But would they occur to us if everything always went well?

During that time of great trouble in my life, I came to have torrid doubts about God, faith, the Scriptures, and truth. I asked, "Is this the way God loves us?" Thus, I had to grapple with the issue, "What is love?"

When my emotions and inner life careened into a barbed wire mesh of misery, I had to ask, "Can't God help? Isn't He is control?" Thus, I was forced to find out what Scripture said about God's sovereignty and how He answers prayer.

When all the good feelings disappeared, I had to proceed in life on raw faith. But faith in what? I found that my faith had long been built on happiness and inner contentment. But when these were stripped away, I was forced to confront these questions: what do I believe? why do I believe it? I began to dig in Scripture to find out what the Word really says about the deity of Christ, the Virgin Birth, the Resurrection, the inspiration of God's Word. In the research I did—trying to hold onto faith like a man holding a thin cord in a hurricane—a foundation of faith was laid that was built on truth and facts, not feelings.

When we confront these issues, our spiritual lives are deepened and broadened. By plowing through them and wrestling with the spectres of darkness, we emerge on the other side with a loyalty and a love for God that is eternal.

Seeing Who He Was

As Job wrestled with these questions, he discovered something else: no matter what he did, he couldn't change his situation. He was totally at the mercy of God.

Job prayed, wept, and screamed at God. In 16:6 he said, "If I speak, my pain is not lessened, and if I hold back, what has left me?" In other words, "No matter what I do, nothing changes." In 19:8 he cries, "He has walled up my way so that I cannot pass; and He has put darkness on my paths." Job's happy sashay through life was suddenly interrupted. He had to face God and who he was—a small, weak human who could do nothing without God.

Why? Why does God allow things to happen that we are powerless to change? And when we cry to Him, why does He sometimes do nothing?

We tend to think God is almost heartless. But what was really happening? Job was learning true humility. He was discovering that God indeed was Lord—that He could do anything with Job just as He pleased, and Job couldn't say a thing about it.

Does that sound harsh?

Maybe it does. But it's essential to begin thinking this way. Only through experiencing the power of God do we realize that we are powerless and must rely on Him. Only through seeing the authority of God will we bow before Him in humility and submission. Only through facing His sovereignty in our lives will we admit, "He is Lord and I must obey Him."

A friend came to me in turmoil over his marriage. He told me he didn't love his wife anymore. He wanted out. I said, "You can't do that. You made a vow before God."

He said he didn't care.

I said God would hold him to his vow and never grant him true life if he knowingly disobeyed it.

"You mean God would do that?" He was incredulous.

"Absolutely."

"You mean I have no choice in the matter?"

"No. You do have a choice to obey God or not. Which will it be?"

He bowed his head. "If I choose to disobey Him, I may lose everything. But if I obey, I'm miserable."

I said, "If you obey, God will fill your life with every good thing spiritually."

"You mean it?"

I meant it.

It's such a hard lesson. We think obedience is based on good feelings. It's not. It's based on a choice made from a heart of faith. Feelings follow that choice.

It was the same for Job. For he said at the end, "I know that You canst do all things, and that no purpose of Yours can be thwarted" (42:2). He bowed before the Almighty and recognized God's absolute right to sovereignty and authority.

Does God Owe Us Something?

When this transformation occurred in Job, something else happened. He began to see that God didn't owe him anything.

For many long hours he argued with his friends, saying that he was righteous and God shouldn't be doing this to him: "God has wronged me" (19:6). "As God lives, who has taken away my right . . . I hold fast my righteousness and will not let it go" (27:2, 6). Job felt that because he was a good man, God owed it to him to bless him.

He didn't always feel this way. For at the beginning of his trial, he said, "The Lord gave and the Lord has taken away. Blessed be the name of the Lord" (1:21). But as the trial persisted without respite, Job was worn down. He told himself and his friends, "I don't deserve this!"

Do you ever find yourself doing that? Maybe the boss drills you through with some strong words, and you go out to your friends, tell them about it, and they say, "You shouldn't have to put up with that." Or your spouse gets upset and screeches about some injustice, but you harden your eyes and say, "I'm not going to listen to this. I'm getting out of here!" Or maybe the kids get on your nerves after a long day and finally you explode, "I'm not going to stand for another minute of this stuff!"

Everybody owes it to us! But what do they owe? To be nice. Not to mess with our reverie. To keep cool. Not to make demands. We have so many rights strewn around our psyches that when any one of them is pulverized by some unfeeling person (man or God), we're outraged.

But when all Job's complaints were through and God finally spoke from the whirlwind, Job said, "Behold, I am insignificant; what can I reply to Thee? I lay my hand on my mouth" (40:4). Job realized he had no right to complain, no right to scream at God.

What had God taught him? The meaning of God's grace. Grace says that everything we have—our brains, our wealth, our families, our heritage, or whatever we consider important—is a gift from God. "What do you have that you did not receive?" asked Paul (1 Corinthians 4:7). Grace means that God pours out the riches of His blessings on us, and we haven't deserved a droplet. We haven't done anything to merit, warrant, or cause it. It's all because He alone is gracious. Grace means, ultimately, that we have every reason to be filled with gratitude.

Sometimes I've heard people say, "Why should I be thankful? Everything I have I've gotten by my own work."

Really? Did you get your mental abilities? Were you the one who created your talent for music? If you were placed in a field with nothing but dirt, what could you create on your own? And even the dirt would be a gift!

Real gratitude—for life, for good things, for joy, for hope, for every good gift we have—comes only as we see God's grace. When God spoke from the whirlwind, suddenly Job saw it. Everything he had was from God. Now he could give thanks with all his heart. Now he could worship God with all his soul, mind, and might. Now he could serve Him with abandon.

No Answers Elsewhere

Even with all these wonderful results, there is more. Job also discovered that man has no answers to the issues that tear our hearts out; only God can give the answers that satisfy.

What was Job doing with his friends from chapters three through thirty-one? Asking questions. But like an old machine with an unoiled gear, his friends kept grinding out the wrong answers.

Job asked, "Why is this happening to me?"

His friends said, "Because you've sinned." And Job refuted it.

Job asked, "Where is God? Why won't He help me?"

They said, "Because you won't repent." He refuted it.

Job asked, "What good is it to serve God if this happens to a good man?"

They answered, "It's not happening to a good man. You're a despicable sinner." Job refuted it again.

To be sure, people have given answers to such questions throughout the ages. But only one kind of answer really satisfies: the answer God gives in His Word.

During my search for faith, before I was born again in August, 1972, I was known in my fraternity as "the sage." If anyone wanted a philosophical discussion, all he had to do was bound into my room and proceed. One evening a friend of mine and I discussed what happens when a man dies. He told me that death was the end. You no longer exist.

I said, "But don't you think we're much more than that? That makes living rather meaningless."

He replied, "All we are is the product of chemical reactions in our minds. When the chemistry stops, so do we."

It was an intriguing idea, but wholly unsatisfying.

When Gertrude Stein died, it is said that on her deathbed she murmured, "What is the answer?" A while later, shortly before she passed away, she said, "What is the question?"

I think that capsulizes the plight of man. We seek answers. There are so many questions. But when we face the unknown, we barely know what to ask. And all our speculations, all our contrivances, all our little theories and philosophies do nothing to bring real peace and hope.

Yet when we take one word from Jesus—"In my Father's house are many dwelling places"—a multitude of issues are settled, and we can lay back, quiet and content.

As Job asked his burning questions, he discovered that man had no answers. *None.* But when he saw God and learned from Him the truth, it was all settled.

Do you see the Word of God as the only source of truth that matters? Certainly mankind has discovered some wonderful things about the nature of our world through scientific inquiry and discovery. We know how to split atoms, how bees dance to direct their comrades to the honey, and how to perform a bypass on a person who would otherwise die in five years. But these are all surface things. How to transform a criminal into a gentleman; how to help a couple to live in mutual understanding and love; how to make peace between nations that lasts—all these elude us.

Yet, let a person plunge into Romans or Ephesians. Let him memorize the words and milk the truth till he grows. Let him apply those truths to the daily problems of life. And you will see all those things and more come to pass.

Job's struggle led him to an important conclusion: God's Word is truth; It transforms; His Word is all I have in this world to hang onto.

Have you come to that place? It can only come when you are forced to hold it like a man holding the rail of a ship in a monsoon.

Satan Disproved Once and For All
Consider another "good" that came out of Job's suffering: Satan's

conviction that people only serve God for what He gives them was dismantled as bunk. Do you know, in fact, that Satan hates people who stick with God despite their suffering more than any other? "Humble yourselves under the mighty hand of God, that He may exalt you at the proper time . . . Be of sober spirit, be on the alert; your adversary, the devil, prowls about like a roaring lion seeking someone to devour. But resist him, knowing that the same experiences of suffering are being accomplished by your brethren who are in the world" (1 Peter 5:6–9). Satan longs to devour any of us.

But God won't let him. Instead, God will cause our suffering to yield up a crop of glory like no other (2 Corinthians 4:1–15).

Any person who refuses to give in and who obeys despite his pain is one more link in the chain that will bind Satan to hell for all eternity. His lie dies every time a saint says, "Father, I thank You for all that has happened for I know that You're turning it all for good." His deceptions wither away as each Christian sings in his pain. Rejoicing Christians are God's proofs against the biggest lies in history.

A Vision of God

Beyond all these things, there is one last thing that happened from which Job would never recover: he saw God as He was.

In the vision out of the whirlwind, God revealed His wisdom, power, knowledge, grace, goodness, justice, and perfection to Job. For the first time, Job really saw God. He saw that God was so much greater, wiser, stronger, and bigger than he was that all he could say at the end was, "I retract, and I repent in dust and ashes" (42:6).

That is always the end of the troughs: we come to see God. At the end of each trough, He looks a little bigger, a little greater than ever before.

C.S. Lewis's *Chronicles of Narnia* contain some of the finest insights into the person of God of any books I know. One of his best is in *Prince Caspian* where the little girl, Lucy, meets Aslan (who represents Christ). She cries, "Aslan, you're much bigger."

Aslan replies, "That is because you are older, little one."

"Not because you are?"

"I am not. But every year you grow, you will find me bigger" (p. 136).

What an insight! It's as we grow in the troughs that God grows in our hearts and fills them. We begin to see Him as He truly is, not as we imagined Him.

One Final Good

There's one other good that came through all this: the Book of Job itself. What a blessing that book is to hurting people. Once and for all Job proves that we don't all hurt because of our own mistakes or sins. Those so quick to judge and point out sin are silenced before Job. They will be silenced before us as well.

Consider the many great books that have come out of suffering:

—The letters to the Romans, Philippians, Ephesians, Colossians, Timothy, and Philemon—all written while in prison.

—*Pilgrim's Progress,* the second bestseller of all time (behind the Bible), written by John Bunyan while in prison.

—The German Bible, translated from the Greek and Hebrew by Martin Luther while hiding in Wartburg castle from the pope.

—Alexander Solzhenitsyn's books written in the gulag.

—So many others.

Then there's Job. Does it have new power for you?

Things to Think About or Discuss:

1. How have you seen Romans 8:28 work out in the trials you've experienced? How did you feel about that passage during the trial? Before? After?

2. Which "good" that came for Job do you consider the greatest good?

3. What "goods" would you like to see come out of trials in your life? How much are you willing to suffer in order to gain those "goods"?

4. How do you think God tailors suffering for each person? Does He use a special plan for each? What do you think would move you most to change?

12
You Can Triumph!

One day you're sitting on the veranda sipping your iced tea. Suddenly, one of the neighbors runs up. "Harry, it's your son. There's been an accident."

You rush off down the street. In your hurry, you trip on the curb, fall on your face, break your nose, and suffer a concussion. Six months later you wake up in the hospital hurting all over. The nurse explains. "Well sir, I don't know how to explain all this. Your son and daughter were killed in a car wreck. Your business burned down and they discovered the insurance wasn't paid. Then a gasoline truck ran off the street and barreled into your house and blew up. There's nothing left. They expect there will be a long battle in the courts."

You stare glassily at the lady and murmur, "What about my wife?"

"Well, that's another thing. She couldn't bear the pressure and apparently has left. No one can find her."

"Are my parents okay?"

"I didn't think you'd want to know all this so soon, but when they got the news, both immediately suffered strokes and now they're confined to a nursing home."

You slump further into your covers.

"Is there anything else?"

"Yes. Just one more thing. I'm very sorry about this one, but it's the rules. It's very fortunate you've awakened, because your health insurance ran out today and we don't know who will pay the bills. You'll have to be removed from the hospital."

"Where to?"

"Anywhere you want."

"I repeat, 'Where to?' "

"I'm very sorry. I didn't think I'd be the one on duty when you came out of your coma."

You reflect a moment. Finally you say, "Just one other question, Ma'am."

"Yes."

"Why did all this happen to me?"

"Oh, dear," says the nurse. "I knew you'd ask something like that and that's why I've prepared an answer. You can read about it all in the Book of Job." She stares expectantly at her patient.

You murmur, "That's real comforting, lady," then turn over on your bed and face the wall. "How long do I have before they remove me?"

"About half an hour. Will that be enough?"

Enough? Can anything be enough after all that?

I doubt that such a scenario will ever take place anywhere. But when you hurt, it doesn't matter what level the pain is on—whether it's emotional, physical, financial, or spiritual. It hurts. You're the one who hurts. And you'd like to know what to do about it.

What help does Job offer all of us who seem to go from problem to problem, calamity to calamity, often with little insight, hope, encouragement, or fortitude?

What Can We Expect?

Probably the first question one should ask is what to expect if we go through a period of personal turmoil and strife—the classical "dark night of the soul"?

Using Job as our model, here are several thoughts.

1. Whatever comes—calamity, illness, spiritual dryness, doubt, pain, loss—will appear to have happened by wholly natural causes. Everything that happened to Job and his family looked like purely normal circumstances. They only become abnormal because they happened on such a monstrous scale and so closely together. Thus, while such testing might look normal and natural, its proportions will signal that it's not just circumstance, happenstance, or coincidence.

2. For a period we will seek an explanation—"Did I sin?"; "Is God punishing me?"; "Why is God doing this to me?"—but we will not find a satisfying answer. We'll begin asking everyone, reading books, trying to find some secret or magic truth that will terminate our agony. But nothing will help.

3. We will gain little comfort from anyone, including God. In fact, He will seem to have vanished. His "presence"—the sixth inner sense all Christians gain when they're reborn by which we know He's with us—will be distant, if not impossible to grasp.

4. We will be troubled by doubts and a constant pressure to "give up our faith," to give up believing that Jesus existed, was and is the Son of God, died for our sins, and reigns in heaven. We will be forced to study the Scriptures to convince ourselves Christianity is true, our salvation is real, and our faith is genuine.

5. In particular, people may start out trying to be encouraging and comforting, but eventually they'll try to tell us we must have sinned in some way. This will be especially hard to bear, since we will be searching our minds and hearts every day, combing the ground for the slightest infractions. But nothing certain will be apparent.

6. We will become obsessed with our pain, thinking only about getting away from it, and pleading with God for answers that do not come. Many of our friends will begin to avoid us because we're such a "downer" to be around.

7. Some people will stick by us. Perhaps only one or two, and probably someone who has gone through a similar trial and seems to have a special understanding of our condition.

8. God will let us continue in our condition without giving us His answers for a limited period. It may be weeks, months, even years. But the time is limited.

9. God will come and release us from our trial, bringing greater blessing afterwards than we ever imagined.

10. Last, we may never know in this life why it all happened. Job never learned the explanation offered in the first pages of his book.

You can be sure that even now Satan has his lawyers and advocates in God's throne room seeking to get an opportunity against you. If you're walking with God, God's hedge is up around you. For your sake and the kingdom's sake, God may open the hedge a crack to test you, to see whether you're the real thing, to prove once and for all that you're His and no one can say anything to the contrary.

This is not meant to be scary. God doesn't want us plodding through life wondering when He'll let the hammer fall. His promise is that He'll see us through to the conclusion. What He started, He intends to finish (Philippians 1:6).

But it is possible that you or I may soon be plunged into a trial so serious and devastating that we literally become contemporary Jobs. What principles or helps might we find along the way?

Some Handholds
As I muddled through those days of turmoil back in 1975 through 1978, it seemed that simply getting through the day was victory enough. I meandered along, or should I say, staggered along, wondering what new plague would erupt into my consciousness. I lived with fear, pain, doubt, and a constant urge to commit suicide.

Looking back, it's easy enough to offer my insights. I'm past it, and the darkness no longer grips my mind and heart like it did back then. I confess to you that I did not do well. I gave up every hour. I wept repeatedly. To my friends I became the ultimate "bummer." I complained, questioned, grilled, and argued with them about what was happening constantly. The only subject I ever wanted to talk about was depression and how to get out of it.

Yet I can see that the Lord continued to be faithful and provided a number of handholds that kept me alive through the darkest period of my life.

Family. Like never before, I leaned on my parents. They became my chief advisors and friends. For the previous three years after becoming a Christian I'd been very hard on them about our differences in faith. But when the depression struck, I found them faithful. They didn't give up on me, even though I gave up on myself. Several times I said to them, "Why don't you just put me in a mental institution?" They replied, "Honey, we love you and know that this period in your life will pass. We aim to see you through it until then." We became close again, for the first time since I became a Christian. I trusted them, their judgment, their wisdom, their love. As awful as my feelings were, it was a time of renewal in our relationship.

Christians. One Sunday I stood up in my church. I was a student in seminary and most of them knew it. We had a "sharing service" going on and several had offered vibrant testimonies of God's love and kindness. When I stood, I said, "What I have to say will not sound good next to these glowing words we've listened to. But over the last weeks and months I've gone through such a terrible time of depression I don't know whether God even exists. I feel as though I've lost my faith in Jesus completely. I'm driven to think of suicide constantly. I've done everything I can think of to deal with the problem, but nothing works anymore. Please pray for me."

That afternoon and week I received numerous letters and words of encouragement. One friend said, "Mark, I appreciated your words last Sunday. You spoke for many who don't have the courage to speak. You're keeping us all honest."

Throughout that period God's people nurtured, strengthened, and built me up. Some waded through the murk with me. One young couple spent days with me talking, taking me places, strengthening me, assuring me. They seemed more committed to me than I was!

Doctors. One of my greatest struggles was the idea that I had seen and was seeing a psychiatrist because of my condition. I felt emasculated, a half man.

Yet I found that it was nothing to be ashamed of. If I had a need, albeit a medical one, there was no reason for me to astigmatize myself about it. If others put me down, so be it. That was their problem.

In this regard, it's important to go to a doctor you trust if your need is psychological. Ask your friends or pastor who they think would be helpful.

It's also of paramount importance that you obey your doctor's orders. My biggest problem here was taking the medication my doctor prescribed. He believed my problem was biochemical. He told me the medication only worked when taken regularly. Yet I developed an obsession with getting off the medication as soon as possible. As a result, whenever I felt better I stopped. This plunged me right back into the same depression I'd been having.

Although the medication was not that effective, I needed to learn to submit myself to my doctor's guidance.

A journal. A great help was keeping a journal, recording insights, victories, changes, encouragements. The very act of having to articulate my feelings was cleansing and healing. I often reread the words at a low moment just to refuel that lonely, hopeful spark that burned within me. It became a place to pray, talk to the Lord, hash through fears, announce resolutions, confess sins. I read back through the passages now and am amazed at how much I wrote and how often God gave me insights I would never have realized on my own.

Expect to get well. My doctor told me that 95% of depressed people don't expect to get well ever again—even though 99.9% of them do. (Of course, right then I put myself in the .1% category!)

Still, most depressing of all was the thought that this was "it" for me for the rest of my life. It's the same with other calamities. The man with financial problems becomes convinced he'll never wade out of it. The couple with marital difficulties sees no end but divorce. But that's a lie of Satan that must be countered. God is not in the defeat business.

Ask questions. One of the things the devil loves to do is to use an idea or unknown to knock us to pieces. When I first visited my doctor, he told me I had an "obsessive-compulsive personality." The moment he said it, I became convinced I was headed for the psychological boonies. "I'm a nut case," I told myself. "You're obsessive-compulsive—totally out of control. Soon you'll be washing your hands forty times a day!"

Then I began to ask questions and my doctor calmed me. I found out he was using psychological terminology for one of ten personality types that have nothing to do with mental illness. "Even Paul was obsessive-compulsive," he said. "There are lots of people with that personality type in the Bible." By finding out the truth, my mind was freed from speculations that would have led me into further darkness.

Other norms. If necessary, check your diet, exercise level, and all the other areas that can normally affect your outlook on life. Make sure you're eating right, sleeping enough, exercising, and spending time in rest and relaxation.

If your problem is depression, like mine was, it could be biochemical. If that is so, no amount of quiet times, verse memorization, prayer, or church-going will help. You need medical attention.

What If I'm *Still* Depressed?

Just the same, a person can take advantage of all of these elements of life and still persist in a soul-ravaging trial that looks eternal. I myself wondered if I'd still be depressed in heaven. It occurred to me that I might have something even God couldn't fix!

That's where another element comes into play which is the most critical of all: God's Word.

Ultimately, the only source of real hope, insight, wisdom, and truth that we have in this world is the Bible. You can study research papers, books, statistics, opinion surveys, and whatever other sources of help that are available. But nothing has the power of God's Word.

That doesn't mean the Word is a magic genie. Just repeat a verse and zipzap—you're back to normal. But rigorous, steady, consistent, and determined application of God's Word reaps results. God has not spoken simply to give us good quotes to throw into our various conversations. Rather, He's given us a book of truth on which we're to stand just as firmly as rock.

Thus, there are certain passages and promises in Scripture that have proven to me to be the most effective words against the powers of darkness. Yes, you will doubt them, question them, cling to them, then throw them all away in a single minute's pain. But if you are His, ultimately you will hold on.

What are these promises?

Hebrews 13:5. "I will never desert you, nor will I ever forsake you." This verse presents two powerful thoughts. One, God won't *desert* us. The word means to abandon or *give up*. The idea is that God would never throw up His hands and say, "You're hopeless. I've decided to let you go."

The second word is stronger. It means a total abandonment. When Jesus cried on the cross, "My God, My God, why hast Thou forsaken Me?" He was picturing a disownment. God had virtually said, "I can't stand the sight of you. You're filth. I will have to destroy you in hell."

But God won't depart from us for a moment or an eternity. He is absolutely loyal.

Yet when your feelings are trampling you, this verse seems to mock you. "But I can't feel You, Lord. Where are You? You seem so far away."

What we have to do is get past our feelings and determine that if God's Word says He won't desert us. He won't. We stake our lives on His Word, not our present feelings.

This is terrifically difficult to do. It's much easier to listen to your inner mental noise and sink into self-pity, lethargy, anger, and despair. "My situation will never change." "God doesn't care anymore." "I might as well die." "I've lost my salvation."

The thing to do is talk to your mind. Repeat what the Word says. Even though your feelings say, "No way. He's gone," you continue to cling to this promise that says He will not *ever under any circumstances* forever turn you away. He remains loyal unto death. And He can never die!

Romans 8:28. "We know that God causes all things to work together for good, for those who love God, for those who are called according to His purpose."

Again Satan can use this verse to mock us. "So you think God can turn even this situation for good? Ha! Show me how."

"Well, I've been reading the Word more."

"And doubting it more, too. You're hopeless. Anyway, how can you say you love God when just yesterday you were screaming at Him that all His promises are bunk!"

"I didn't mean it."

"It sure sounded like you did."

"I repented of it."

"But you did it again this morning."

"He forgives seventy times seven."

"You've done this one well over 490 times. I've been counting."

"That's not what that verse means."

"What does it mean then? You don't even know where it is."

"I do too." You go to your Bible, leaf through it, and give up.

"See. Anyway, how do you know you're one of His called ones? Seems to me your confession of faith was little more than a need for a father figure."

It goes on and on. Finally, Satan will just say, "If God loves you, why are you in this situation?"

You try different answers, but it's the one question that nags at you, too.

Again there needs to be a riveting on His Word, a holding fast. "Even though I don't see it now or understand, I know that You can even use this for good, Lord. I trust You to do that."

You repeat it. You cling to it. You determine to believe it, even if everything in life seems to mock it. "What I'm seeing is not the truth. God's Word is the truth."

Romans 5:3–5. "And not only this, but we also exult in our tribulations, knowing that tribulation brings about perseverance, and perseverance proven character, and proven character, hope, and hope does not disappoint, because the love of God has been poured out in our hearts through the Holy Spirit who was given to us."

Paul says this as he exults in his tribulations. To "exult" does not mean we "take pleasure in" them. It means to "boast, glory in, pride oneself in." For Paul, tribulations were a mark of being a Christian. He'd said to the Philippians, "For to you it has been granted for Christ's sake not only to believe in Him, but also to suffer for His sake" (Philippians 1:29). Later, in chapter three, he said that he wanted "to know Him, and the power of His resurrection, and the fellowship of His sufferings, being conformed to His death" (Philippians 3:1–11).

Peter and John rejoiced "that they had been considered worthy to suffer for Christ's name" (Acts 5:41). Peter himself wrote, "To the degree that you share the sufferings of Christ, keep on rejoicing, so that at the revelation of His glory, you may rejoice with exultation. If you are reviled for the name of Christ, you are blessed, because the Spirit of glory and of God rests upon you" (1 Peter 4:13–14). And Jesus reminded us, "Blessed are those who have been persecuted for the sake of righteousness" (Matthew 5:10). We're to "rejoice and be glad, for our reward in heaven is great" (Matthew 5:12).

Here Paul was reminding us that we "exult" in our tribulations because we see beyond them. We see that they're producing perseverance.

One day in the midst of more turmoil, I said to my roommate, Cliff, "What if I lose my salvation? What if I don't persevere?"

He said, "You're persevering right now."

I didn't understand what he meant. He said, "Look, you still believe and cling to Him even if you doubt, don't you? You haven't renounced Him, have you?"

"No."

"Then you're persevering. How can anyone persevere unless

he has something to persevere through? You'd just be cruising along without thinking about it." That struck me.

I was learning to believe despite my feelings. Tribulation was enabling me to learn to endure.

This quality of perseverance is one of the highest of all virtues in the eyes of God. Jesus was "perfected" through sufferings (Hebrews 2:10). "If we endure, we shall also reign with Him" (2 Timothy 2:12). Endurance is the primary quality of leadership and spiritual maturity. James said, "Consider it all joy, my brethren, when you encounter various trials, knowing that the testing of your faith produces endurance; and let endurance have its perfect result, that you may be perfect and complete, lacking in nothing."

Did you catch that? Perseverance is what leads to perfection and completion. The word for "perfect" means maturity, full adulthood, growing up in the faith. The word for "complete" comes from two roots which mean a "full or whole portion." God doesn't want any element of His character to be lacking in our lives. He wants us full and complete, people who exemplify Jesus in every way possible.

But even this is not the end. Tribulation develops perseverance, and "perseverance brings about proven character." Again, the word translated here for "proven character" is interesting. It pictures a state of proof, of one who has been tested and found true.

If a person says he's honest I'll accept it. But if the FBI sets up a scam in which they attempt to bribe him and he refuses, then his character is "proven."

If a karate expert says he can break a brick, that's impressive. But let's see him put his hand where the brick is and break one! That would prove it.

Real character is not shown by high-sounding words and declarations of faith. Rather, it is revealed by going through a test and showing you are what you say you are. If a person says he believes in Jesus, that's good. But if he says he still believes when the Gestapo stands before him and threatens to shoot him in the forehead if he says he believes, then he's proven it. Real character stays in character even at the point of death.

Only through the ultimate trial of the "dark night of the soul" will our true character show. Will we obey and love Him even when nothing goes right, He refuses to bless, and He even seems to have disappeared?

Going on from there, Paul says, "And proven character brings about hope; and hope does not disappoint, because the love of God has been poured out within our hearts through the Holy Spirit who was given to us."

Real hope only comes through testing. Why?

Take a boxer. Suppose he had to go up against the heavyweight champion tomorrow without any training. He'd probably feel hopeless. But what happens when he goes through training and is pummeled left and right so that his stomach gets hard, his punch becomes lethal, and his jaw stays solid? He has hope. "I can win," he says, because he knows he's made it through the rough times.

It's the same for Christians. We don't really have a hope of heaven until we've seen how useless this world is. We never attain to that "Come quickly, Lord Jesus" mentality until we've seen ourselves harden up through trials. Then we *know* He'll see us through because He's already taken us through so much.

Proverbs 3:5–6. "Trust in the Lord with all your heart, and do not lean on your own understanding; in all your ways acknowledge Him, and He will make your paths straight."

This verse might be paraphrased, "Rely on the Lord without wavering and don't listen to your own internal chatter; whatever comes, look to and turn to Him, and He will clear your path of obstacles."

It's so difficult to get away from what our brains tell us in the midst of trials. "You'll never get out of this one." "You're a complete jerk. Don't think you can overcome this problem." "Don't expect God to help you. You got yourself into it; you get yourself out of it."

Some of the gunk that dribbles into our minds in the middle of trials is incredible. It's all lies. We must refuse to listen to it and turn to God's Word where we find the only real objective and complete truth in life.

During my depression my mind told me such things as, "You're a hopeless case." "You're a schizophrenic. Nobody can fix you, not even God." "This is the way it's going to be for the rest of your life." "God can never use you this way." "God's not changing you because He doesn't exist. He's a figment of your imagination."

But taking Proverbs 3:5–6 in stride, I often found myself saying (to my own amazement), "Lord, I don't understand all these things, but I want to trust You with all my heart. Remove these worries from my soul. Let me put it all in Your hands now."

Often, for the moment, my spirit was calmed.

Verses of Hope
There are a multitude of other verses we can turn to.

James 1:5—for those who need wisdom
James 1:13—how God gives us the "crown of life" after we get through a trial
Matthew 28:20—to assure us He is with us
John 16:33—to gain peace in the midst of our circumstances
Philippians 4:6–7—to find freedom from worry
Matthew 6:33–34—to face the day with victory
Philippians 1:6—to find assurance that He'll see us through
Jude 24—to be strengthened to trust Him to bring us to heaven safely
2 Timothy 4:17–18—to find strength for facing whatever comes

Pick up a pocket promise guide or something like that to gain more help and insight.

One More Verse
There's one other verse right out of Job that speaks great hope to my own heart: *Job 13:15*. "Though He slay me, I will hope in Him. Nevertheless, I will argue my ways before Him."

What was Job saying? Just this. "If God chooses to kill me, I'll still trust Him. No matter what happens to me in this life, He remains utterly trustworthy. I'd rather be in His hands than in any other's. But just the same, I'll present my case to Him as effectively as I can."

This is the ultimate cry of all our hearts. There simply is no one else in all of creation that we can trust wholly but God.

I came upon this verse through a Christian friend who was going through a divorce. She said to me, "Why doesn't God convert my husband, Mark? Why is God allowing this to happen? He's the one who says divorce is wrong. Then why doesn't my husband become a Christian?"

I didn't know. I was struggling with the same issues.

Then she jarred me. "You know, though, I still have hope. Even if I have to go through this divorce. I know He's with me just the same. The prayer of my heart is Job 13:15—'Though He slay me, yet I will trust Him.' I don't understand what He's doing or how I can still trust Him through all this. But I do. I know He'll prove true. I'd rather be going through this and be with Him, than to be perfectly happy and not know Him. Just knowing Him is enough."

I went back to seminary still fighting the darkness. One afternoon when I was angry and hurt about all the things that were happening to me, I took a walk down to the local park. As I walked I prayed and argued with God. "Why won't You take me out of this? Why do You let it persist? Why can't I go back to normal?"

I was so upset that I began renouncing Him. "Lord, I don't want anything to do with You anymore. Just leave me alone. I'll find some way in this world. Becoming a Christian was the worst decision of my life." I wanted to hurt Him into doing something about my depression.

But I just sat there and nothing changed. Finally, I repented and wept. "Lord, I can't renounce You. I love You. I have no one else but You. You're my only hope in this world. Don't You understand? Without You I'm nothing. What can I do? I want to serve You, but this depression is destroying me. Please do something.

I feel as though You've discarded me forever."

At that moment, an elderly woman walked up to me and said, "Sir, could you give me fifty cents to buy a Coke?"

I didn't have any money but said I would be glad to go to my room and bring some to her. She pointed to a nursing home across the way. "I live over there," she said, and then wandered off.

I went home, got a dollar bill, and walked back. I went into the nursing home and asked for the woman. The nurse said, "Oh, don't worry about her. Every now and then she gets out and begs people for money to buy soft drinks. She loves Coke, but it's not really good for her."

I persisted and finally gave the nurse the dollar to give to her. Then I began walking through the nursing home. People in wheelchairs were everywhere. Some reached out their hands to touch me, and pleaded with tired eyes. One said, "Please take me home!" Several asked me to pray with them and read them Bible verses. I sat out in the foyer and talked with some of the men, even engaging one in a lively discussion about what it meant to serve the Lord. One man tried to speak to me, but his voice always seemed to catch and he couldn't get anything out. He was crumpled up in a wheelchair and appeared ready to cry. He put his hand on mine and just left it there. Suddenly I felt I had to do something for these hurting people.

Later that week, I got together a few students and we came to the home and sang. The people just sat there, many of them asleep. But as we played, there was one who began moving his feet. Another clapped his hands to the music. A third brightened and a lively smile beamed on her face. She laughed and said, "This is fun." One woman came up and asked us to do "Amazing Grace."

We sang. Loud, at first. But then we noticed something. Their mouths were moving. We toned down.

And then we heard them—they were singing, too. These lonely, forgotten people were singing in their crackly, raspy voices. *Amazing Grace*. It was the best rendition I ever heard.

After that, I stood up to preach a brief message. I told a joke, and a few laughed. I noticed one man with a huge smile and just a few teeth. He was radiant. I began to preach a message on faith and hope. I told them this nursing home wasn't the end, that God has not destined us to end life in worn-out bodies that don't work anymore. He has promised something far greater. I said, "You can have great hope in Jesus Christ because one day, if you believe, He will give you a home in heaven." I was astonished that they listened.

We sang another song, then moved out among the people, shaking hands, praying. One woman shook my hand warmly and said, "You have renewed my hope."

Afterwards, one of the students asked me, "Where did you learn to preach like that?"

"Like what?" I said.

"Like some kind of flaming evangelist."

I went home that night and wept. Even in the midst of my depression, God had let me serve. I was amazed, uplifted, grateful.

"Though He slay me, yet will I trust Him."

Things to Think About or Discuss:

1. How have people responded to you during your times of trial? Would you want them to respond that way again?

2. What principles or truths do you hold onto the hardest when you go through trials? How much use do you make of God's people? Why do you rely on them the way you do? Or why not?

3. During a trial, do you turn to Scripture? Why or why not?

4. What Scriptures are most helpful to you when you're hurting? What Scriptures would you recommend to a person going through:

> financial problems?
> spiritual problems?
> emotional problems?
> sickness?
> terminal disease?

13
In God's Hands— Always

I have a fear. A great fear. It's this: that someday somewhere I'll plummet again into that darkness that enveloped me from 1975 to 1978, and I won't know how long it will last.

Several times over the years I've felt the tremors of depression shaking back over my soul. But always, after a few hours, it recedes.

Yet, I must confess, I fear it. Could it ever happen again?

I don't know. But does it matter? What good will constricting my gut about it do?

So most of the time I don't think about it. But every now and then . . .

What About You?
You've read this far and maybe you're a little frightened. Maybe you wonder if Satan won't haul off and clobber you tomorrow.

Or this afternoon. Or the next minute.

It can happen. You can't prevent it. You're entirely in the hands of God on this matter.

The infinitely loving God.

The perfectly wise God.

The holy, holy, holy God.

The omnipotent and sovereign God.

Do you think you can trust Him?

Job did. "Though He slay me, yet will I trust Him."

Remarkable words. Can you say them? Maybe something like this: "Lord, it doesn't matter what happens to me in this world. Whatever comes, I know that You are Lord and Master of everything. No one, nothing can touch me apart from Your will. I know that You're good, and will only do what You know is best for me. I know that You're omniscient, and therefore know every detail beforehand. I know that You're kind, and would do nothing that would bring harm to my soul. And I know that You're sovereign; You're in complete control from beginning to end. Therefore, I'll trust You."

Can you say that?

In the end, all of us will have traversed many dark paths. Each of us has a story to tell. Some of it is dark. Some of it is light, filled with fun and laughter. It's our story, nobody else's. But it's also His story—of how He worked in us.

There's one important thing through it all. Just one thing. Nothing else matters.

Before I tell you, remember this. Job cursed the day he was born. He yelled at God. He challenged Him. "Come down here and let's go to court together, Lord, and I'll make my case and You make Yours." He was angry, sad, unhappy, doubting. He wondered if there was life after death, and in the next breath asserted that he believed that God would come and take him to His heavenly kingdom. He fought with his friends and called them nincompoops, dullards, louts, rotten eggs. In the same breath, he'd plead with them to be kind to him in his suffering. He was up, down, and all around. He was a man who suffered intensely.

160

But despite his pain, his doubts, his loud cries in the night, and his anger, there was one thing about Job that pleased God: Job believed. He stuck with it. He hung in there. He kept the faith.

At the end of his life, Paul wrote something to Timothy that has always thrilled me. He said, "I have fought the good fight; I have finished the course; I have kept the faith" (2 Timothy 4:7). That was also Job. He fought. He finished. He kept the faith. He burned to the end, even if at times there was only a flicker against the dark midnight.

But that was enough.

Has it ever occurred to you that is about all God asks of us? He doesn't say, "Go, convert thousands, and then I'll accept you." He doesn't command us, "Make a million and donate it all to My church. Then I'll think highly of you." He never chides us, "You didn't have a quiet time on January 13, 1954. So I'm throwing you out of heaven!"

No. He says, "Only believe. Without faith, it is impossible to please Me" (Hebrews 11:6).

Faith means conviction. It means obedience. It calls for risk. But ultimately it's just taking God at His Word. Simply saying, "You said it, Lord. That's enough for me. I accept it and I'll obey it."

Job was accepted by God because he believed. He didn't give up his convictions.

To be sure, there were moments when he wondered if there was really life after death. Or even if God was there and heard. There was a time when he so asserted himself that he contended that he was righteous in God's eyes.

But despite his pride, his arrogance, his insults, and his own sin, he believed.

God doesn't ask any more of you, or me. For "All things are possible to him who believes" (Mark 9:23).

A Message That Helped Me

During the time of my own trouble in seminary, I heard a message preached by a seminary student. He spoke about Romans

8:18–39. Let me paraphrase what Paul is writing in my own words.

I look at my own sufferings this way: they're simply not worth comparing to the great things God has planned for us in heaven. In fact, the whole creation is groaning at this very moment for that day, when all of us will be revealed as members of God's family. That's the reason the present world has been subjected to total uselessness—because God was hoping that the whole creation would wake up and be set free from its slavery to sin. The whole creation would get so sick of sin that it would want to join God's family as sons and be truly free. Right now the whole world is groaning and suffering like a woman in labor.

And we also groan because we've tasted of His glory by possessing the Spirit. But we want more! We want to be redeemed, to be sons, to have a new body and live forever with the Lord Himself! We've been saved in that hope. Of course, if we'd already achieved it, if we already had new bodies, why would we still be hoping? Nobody hopes for what he already has! Rather, he hopes for what he doesn't have. And for that reason we wait eagerly for it every day.

At the same time the Spirit Himself helps us in our present weakness. He teaches us to pray, because we don't even know what to pray about. In fact, sometimes, when we can only groan and weep, that's actually the Spirit praying in us. Jesus searches our hearts through the Spirit and then speaks to the Father on our behalf, right up there in heaven. Even now!

That's part of the reason that we know God causes everything to work together for good in our lives—everything—because He's praying to that end. But He prays only for those who love God and for those He's called, not for those who reject Him. God planned that everyone whom He has set His love on will become exactly like Jesus in character, because He wanted Jesus to be only the first among a multitude of brethren. And everyone that He predestined to this purpose He called. Everyone He called, He has made perfectly righteous in His sight. And everyone He made righteous through faith will be glorified with Him in heaven.

Tell me, then, what are we going to say to these things? If God is on our side, who can be against us? If He didn't even spare Jesus, but sent Him to the cross to redeem us, do you think He's going to withhold lesser things from us?

So who's going to charge any one of us with sin? God is the one who made us righteous. So who can condemn us? Jesus? No way. Even now He's at God's right hand speaking on our behalf. He'd never condemn us.

Who then could separate us from God? A trial in this world? A personal problem? Persecution by others? No way. Or how about a famine? Never. Perhaps if we were naked we'd be separated? That's ridiculous. Shall a terrible situation or the threat of death separate us from God? Never in a million years. In fact, He's the one who said that we're being put to death by others in this world for Him, as a way of showing His power to the world.

When believers face death triumphantly, it shows how great He really is! In fact, all these things are merely ways that God enables us to achieve an incredible victory over the flesh, the devil, and the world.

I'm convinced that nothing can ever separate us from God's love—not anything in death or in this life, not an angel in heaven or a demon in hell, not anything present or anything anyone can invent in the future, not any human power. We can't go high or low enough to get away from God. Nothing in all creation can pull us away from His love, which has been demonstrated in Jesus our Lord.

This student showed me that this passage taught two basic things about God. One was that He is absolutely sovereign. He does with us as He pleases. He used an illustration that helped: on his lawn he had a number of little mimosa trees that grew naturally. Every week he went over them with his lawnmower and cut them down. But one summer he decided to plant some of those mimosa trees. Now how was it that sometimes he killed mimosa trees and other times he saved them? The student said,

"I had a perfect right to do that—I'm the sovereign keeper of the yard!"

I could see this very thing happening in my life. God was doing with me as He pleased. At one time, He made my life overflow with joy, love, and peace. But now He was allowing me to go through trouble for purposes only He knew. He was sovereign.

Frankly, it wasn't so comforting. But then he showed how the passage also teaches that God is love. Everything He does is marked by love. He never does anything that isn't loving. He saved us out of love for us, and continues to mold us in a loving fashion.

He shared how his mother had gone through a serious period of mental illness. For several years she wandered in and out of this state, to the grief of all concerned. But his father loved her, retired early, and took care of her. Later, he wrote his children about it. It had been a tough time. The mother would awaken at night and wander about the house, crazy, upset, deranged. She wouldn't recognize him. She would cry out about invisible things that attacked her, hurt her. It was difficult.

But this man wanted his children to know one thing. It wasn't time lost. It wasn't worthless. Through it God had done a work in both their lives. They had both come to know the Lord more intimately and deeply than ever before. He wanted them to know that God's words—"All things work together for good, to those who love God"—were true. They were never more true than when he and his wife were both going through the darkness.

That student's words touched me deeply. Even today, when I listen to the tape, I weep. For this was the very thing happening to me.

He left us with two dramatic statements about suffering. He said, "Remember this as you go through the darkness: God knows; and God cares." He is sovereign over it. And He is loving us through it.

I would like to add something else to that. Not only does God *know* all that we're going through. Not only does He *care deeply* about it. But He is also able to use it to work in us something marvelous—the character of Jesus, a closer relationship with Him, a deeper love for Him, a finer walk with Him.

For that I can live with my fear. I know that God will use everything in life to mold me and make me all that I can be in this world and the next.

I don't know what pain I'll face, or you'll face. But I know this: God knows; God cares; and He will use it for glory.

That's enough to enable me to trust Him forever. What about you?

Things to Think About or Discuss:

1. Do you see the Book of Job ultimately as a source of hope? Why or why not?

2. Has Job become more understandable to you? Do you think it's legitimate to see Job as an example of a kind of trial all of us must go through on some level in our lives? Why or why not?

3. What hope does Romans 8:18–39 offer you? What verses in particular speak to your heart? Explain.

4. How do you think you will respond now if you go through a dark time? What truths, principles, or people will you lean on most? Why? What changes do you see in your own thinking about the problem of suffering?